T0196851

Cambridge Elements ≡

Elements in Publishing and Book Culture
edited by
Samantha Rayner
University College London
and
Rebecca Lyons
University of Bristol

DIGITAL AUTHORSHIP

Publishing in the Attention Economy

R. Lyle Skains
Bangor University

CAMBRIDGE
UNIVERSITY PRESS

CAMBRIDGE
UNIVERSITY PRESS

University Printing House, Cambridge CB2 8BS, United Kingdom

One Liberty Plaza, 20th Floor, New York, NY 10006, USA

477 Williamstown Road, Port Melbourne, VIC 3207, Australia

314–321, 3rd Floor, Plot 3, Splendor Forum, Jasola District Centre,
New Delhi – 110025, India

79 Anson Road, #06–04/06, Singapore 079906

Cambridge University Press is part of the University of Cambridge.

It furthers the University's mission by disseminating knowledge in the pursuit of
education, learning, and research at the highest international levels of excellence.

www.cambridge.org
Information on this title: www.cambridge.org/9781108444484
DOI: 10.1017/9781108649537

First published 2019

A catalogue record for this publication is available from the British Library.

ISBN 978-1-108-44448-4 Paperback
ISSN 2514-8524 (online)
ISSN 2514-8516 (print)

Cambridge Elements

Digital Authorship

Publishing in the Attention Economy

Elements in Publishing and Book Culture

DOI: 10.1017/9781108649537
First published online: January 2019

R. Lyle Skains
Bangor University

Author for correspondence: r.l.skains@bangor.ac.uk

ABSTRACT: This Element looks at contemporary authorship via three key authorial roles: indie publisher, hybrid author, and fanfiction writer. The twenty-first century's digital and networked media allows writers to disintermediate the established structures of royalty publishing and to distribute their work directly to – and often in collaboration with – their readers. This demotic author, one who is "of the people," often works in genres considered "popular" or "derivative." The demotic author eschews the top-down communication flow of author > text > reader, in favor of publishing platforms that generate attention capital, such as blogs, fanfiction communities, and social media.

KEYWORDS: indie publishing, demotic author, fanfiction authorship, hybrid authorship, self-publishing

ISBNs: 9781108444484 (PB), 9781108649537 (OC)
ISSNs: 2514-8524 (online), 2514-8516 (print)

Contents

Introduction

I wrote my first story when I was nine years old. It may, of course, have been my hundredth or thousandth story, for all that I am capable of remembering those long-ago scribblings. I think of this one – a few hundred words, written in the style of my then-favorite author, Judy Blume – as my first simply because I still have it: my fourth-grade teacher, Miss Eileen, typed it up, pressed it into photo album pages, and bound it with ribbon into my very first "book." To me, an avid reader and aspiring writer, this packaging of the words I had written made me something more. It made me an author.

For most of recent memory, to be an author was something subtly but assuredly different from being a writer. A writer could be described as aspiring, freelance, hobbyist, short-form, technical, struggling, copy-, or by any number of other terms that refer to amateur or apprenticed practitioners of the craft. An author, however, was a writer who had "made it": they had their name on the cover of a book, stamped into reverence, respect, and immortality. An author was not only being paid to write (as many writers are) – they held a position of authority. Nonfiction authors gained publishing contracts for being experts or for having singular experiences, making them literal authorities on their topics. Fiction authors achieved authorship by demonstrating superiority in narrative craft: characterization, poetics, emotional effectiveness, and plotting. An entire publishing industry existed to exalt these chosen few; in the aspiring author's mind, receipt of a publishing contract granted them a parade of proofreaders and designers and promoters and book tours and window displays (a fantasy Hollywood thoroughly reinforces).

If such a paradigm ever existed for more than a fractional percentage of authors, it was certainly fleeting, and is now gone. The twentieth-century model of authorship was deeply embedded in a publishing industry that invested highly in an author-centric ideology (Ramdarshan Bold 2016): authors worth publishing are special in some way, enough so that their words mean more than anyone else's, justifying their production, amplification, and sales to millions of readers. This model relies upon a reading-literate society in which the largest proportion by far are *readers* (Laquintano 2016, p. 20), recipients of knowledge and art, rather than generators of such. In this cultural frame, authorial voices are select and selected, the few communicating to the many, in a dominant power structure that reasserts itself with every book printed.

The twenty-first century, however, has ushered in a new era of authorship, thanks to the affordances of digital media and the Internet. Online digital and social media have broken down the barriers between mass communicator and audience, sponsoring a many-to-many communication paradigm through the interactive capabilities of Web 2.0 (O'Reilly 2007). On websites, blogs, newsfeeds, and media streams, a reading-literate culture has transitioned into a writing-dominant culture – and while most bloggers and posters achieve very little in the way of audience numbers, the costs of reaching them are so greatly diminished by digital tools that many have no need of a publisher to package their message. From this cacophony of voices, a new author has emerged, side-stepping the twentieth-century publishing hierarchy to communicate directly to their audience – often via two-way communication. This direct route develops relationships and communities, enabling attention to flow to the author. Some authors and platforms afford conversion of that attention into currency; others actively reject such a transition, instead bartering in a gift economy of writing and cultural exchange.

I have termed this breed of author the *demotic author*: one who is "of the people," participating in a community of writers and readers, often in genres considered "popular," common, or even denounced as derivative and of lesser worth. The demotic author eschews the top-down communication flow of author → text → reader in favor of publishing platforms that permit and encourage feedback and conversation, such as blogs, fanfiction communities, and social media. In fact, the demotic author relies upon these platforms to generate attention for themselves and their work, often in lieu of the attention generated by a publishing house's marketing machine. They proliferate and thrive in a writing-literate culture; often, their method of writing and publishing is an alternative avenue toward expressing their voice, as the twentieth-century royalty model silences so many. The demotic author is both a re-emergence of oral storytellers of old, walking amongst their audiences and responding to them, and a figure of the future, when publishing spheres may not be controlled by the few, but shared spaces for the many.

The Rise of the Demotic Author

Timothy Laquintano aptly describes the current and rising trend of self-publishing as *mass authorship*: "multiple viable models of publishing have emerged to compete and complement one another; these multiple models force us to consider publishing both as a professional practice and as a literacy practice accessible to everyday people" (2016, pp. 6–7). Mass authorship arises in a writing-literate culture, where writing becomes an everyday practice and a dominant form of labor, and in which the social role of the writer is emphasized and embraced over the social role of the reader (Brandt 2015). It is afforded by technologies that evolve the book from a *read-only* medium to a *read-write* medium, converting a static object into a conceptual foundation for a community to converse, share, and respond creatively to its ideas, characters, and environs (cf. Lessig 2008). When writing – including communicating through text messages and publishing through social media – is a more dominant and desirable[1] form of activity than

---

[1] A 2015 YouGov survey identified *authors* and *librarians* as the most desirable professions, at 60 percent and 54 percent of the respondents, respectively. No other category except *academic* scored over the 50 percent mark (51%).

reading, when platforms and tools exist not to merely deliver content but to easily create and share it, when one can be assured of quick and easy feedback in the form of shares and likes and comments, then almost everyone can perceive themselves as having a voice worthy of publication and amplification. The romanticised notion of the author, a writer of divine inspiration and original genius, crumbles when readers realize that they, too, have something to say, no matter how mundane, and that they have the ability to say it to someone who might listen.

That is not to say, of course, that an author-centric ideology does not persist. Brandt's writing-oriented literacy co-exists in a culture that continues to formally promote reading-oriented literacy; likewise, new models of writing and publishing are emerging even as the royalty[2] publishing system continues to dominate, though diminished from its twentieth-century prominence (Laquintano 2016). Ironically, while the self-published and hybrid authors I discuss in sections 1 and 2 have at least partially discarded notions of Romantic authorship, fanfiction writers (section 3) practice their craft in a tenuous space of legitimacy that leads them to firmly uphold nineteenth- and twentieth-century notions of authorship, ownership, and copyright just so they won't be noticed enough for their work to be shut down, whether legally or culturally. Nonetheless, fans have emerged from the shadows into the sunny, exposed locales of the Internet, connecting with one another to the point of legitimizing their communities, if not always their writing. They are a key example of how power has transitioned from authors and publishers to

---

[2] I use the term *royalty publishing* throughout this Element to refer to what we commonly think of as "traditional publishing": the royalty-based publishing model that dominated the twentieth century, particularly in terms of fiction, as opposed to government, religious, or author-subsidized publishing. This definition is drawn from Laquintano 2016.

audiences and readers through their reviews, commentary, and sharing, making them influential players in the literary field of cultural production (Pecoskie and Hill 2015, p. 621; Ramdarshan Bold 2016).

Fanfiction writers are also a key example of Internet culture, where value is generated not necessarily from the exchange of currency, but through the exchange of information and content (Carolan and Evain 2013). While fanfic writers trade exclusively in a gift economy (Currah 2007) – content for content, feedback for feedback – other demotic authors dip into this prosumer space in novel ways that enable them to trade content for attention, and convert attention into currency. Authors can reach readers through social media, generating connections that, while they may not be *actual* relationships, nonetheless carry the *illusion* of such for their followers. They engage in forums, post YouTube videos, and have active Twitter, Facebook, and Tumblr feeds, sharing some of their work (and often, their hobbies, beliefs, and personal lives) for free in order to generate attention for their published work. Content alone is increasingly less significant to consumers, particularly as so much is available on the web for free; demotic authors have found bartering attention provides something of what users are looking for, helping them convert casual followers into dedicated fans and patrons (cf. Carolan and Evain 2013, p. 295).

The rise of the demotic author has been driven in part by the difficulties the royalty publishing industry has faced in the past few decades. The lumbering behemoths (often noted as the "Big 5": Hachette, HarperCollins, Macmillan, Penguin Random House, and Simon & Schuster) that grew out of the twentieth century saw their audience fracture with the popularity of film, games, and the Internet in particular as a conveyor of free content. Royalty publishers found their established practices and methods of production and dissemination weakened (Tian and Martin 2011, p. 234). Rather than innovating their content or their delivery system (as, for example, Allen

Lane's Penguin did with paperbacks in the 1930s), royalty publishers shifted their focus to bestsellers and known authors – sure, marketable bets (Ramdarshan Bold 2016, p. 3). There has been a significant decline in the number and size of royalty advances since 2008 (Gibson, Johnson, and Dimita 2015, p. 5); it is no coincidence that this trend began shortly after the implementation of the Kindle and the Kindle Direct Publishing (KDP) platform in 2007. This practice strengthened the barriers to entry to new authors and made it increasingly difficult for midlist authors to persist, resulting in a large community of unpublished writers disillusioned with royalty publishers just as technologies and marketplaces were emerging to offer them alternative routes.

The technologies and cultures of the Internet, from social media to ecommerce, have enabled a resurgence in the practice and the reputation of self-publishing (which I will primarily refer to as "indie publishing"). New technologies of the ebook, epublishing, and online booksellers' search algorithms provide value to content (Thompson 2012, p. 339) – including low barriers to entry, ease of access, updatability, searchability, portability, flexibility, affordability, and even intertextuality and multimedia – that enable these indie publishers to effectively replace the value-added services (editing, typesetting, printing, distribution) that once made royalty publishing the sole marker of quality. As Thompson notes, commercial fiction has been a significant driver for the rise of ebooks (ibid., p. 322); so-called "popular" fiction writers have eagerly embraced the affordances of new technologies to develop their texts and reach their audiences without the limitations of the slow and increasingly selective royalty system. Effectively, they are disintermediating royalty publishers and their linear model of publication (Murray 2010, p. 26) in favor of a more participatory and attention-based model that emphasizes many-to-many communication and long-tail economics (Hillesund 2007). Likewise, their readers have responded, disregarding the publishing method of texts (if they even are aware of them; Amazon and others make little distinction between royalty- and indie-published texts) in favor of more and diverse content (Carolan and Evain 2013, p. 298). Further, indie publishing has permitted small publishers and authors to experiment with their work, crossing genres, returning to the short forms to suit commuters, and reaching niche audiences (Dietz 2015, p. 206).

The book- and author-based communities that arise in this demotic publishing model are part of the emergence of a new era of communicative culture, as the secondary oral culture (Ong 1982 [2005]) of the Internet's social media and Web 2.0 interfaces propagates a writing-literate culture (Brandt 2015) in which everyone is a published author with a potential audience. This culture affords both "legitimate" writing (defined by Laura Dietz as paid, usually with a royalty advance) and "illegitimate" writing, including blogging, online discourse on social media and forums, new experimental forms such as collaborative wiki novels, and indie publishing (Dietz 2015, p. 202). Thus Laquintano offers a comprehensive definition of publishing as a literary practice: that which "develops under conditions in which ordinary people have the ability to publish their writing using digital infrastructures" (2016, p. 12). Under such a definition, we are all authors, publishing every time we update a status on Facebook or comment on a news article. Under such a definition, indie publishers and even fanfiction writers are no less legitimized than royalty publishers.

The Attention Economy

The demotic author's publication practices have been afforded and legitimized by digital media and culture, yet they still face the same hurdles of any content producer: marketing to and reaching their audience. As multiple media have proliferated, and the information superhighway has become more of a content galaxy, consumer attention is fractured and fleeting.

Thanks to the easy replicability of digital content, the power of search engines, and the continual development of personalized product recommendation algorithms (a harbinger of the semantic web's intelligent applications), the difficulties of publishing are no longer in creating and distributing content but in discoverability in an age of hyperabundance (Bhaskar 2013; Goldhaber 1997; Laquintano 2016; Thompson 2012). When everyone is a publisher – not just of books, but of content across the whole of the Internet – *attention* becomes the scarcest resource (Goldhaber 1997), and "those who can gather and create attention are the new bankers of an *attention economy*" (Bhaskar 2013, p. 177, emphasis mine).

In the royalty publishing model, attention is garnered through the publisher's marketing machine: distribution to and display in bookshops, advertisements, critics' reviews, book club adoption, and placement on best-seller lists (which can be manipulated [Miller 2000]). Indie publishers, such as those discussed in section 1, have no such marketing might, and thus must utilize other means, including the "embeddedness" of economic behavior and institutions within networks of social relations (Miller 2006, p. 9); writers who seek an audience no longer have the luxury of fulfilling the romanticised role of author, remote and above commercial and financial concerns (Phillips 2014, p. 7). Hybrid authors, as discussed in section 2, have significantly more attention, as they build on that gained through their royalty publishing streams, adding to it with their independent epublishing activities and social/online interactions. Fanfiction writers (section 3), notably, have somewhat different goals when it comes to audiences; many perceive reader attention as secondary to their primary motivation: to respond to, participate in, and reshape an existing story for their own satisfaction. For these authors, attention is a bonus, and as they have little to no expectation of monetizing any attention they gain, they trade almost exclusively in attention rather than attempting to convert it to currency.

Indie and hybrid authors, like any public figure, do not barter attention like-for-like; they are not as deeply invested in each of their followers/readers as their followers are in them. What they offer their followers is *illusory attention*: an unequal offering that nonetheless leads the receiver to feel they are being granted more attention than they actually are (Goldhaber 1997, n.p.). Likes, shares, and occasional direct replies to followers contribute to this form of attention, as do activities such as rewarding crowdfunding backers with special content (a key contributor to the success of patronage platforms). Particularly in the secondary oral culture of the Internet, followers can see the author's attention to *other* followers, and thus this increases the illusion that each one individually is receiving attention. The followers subsequently become amplifiers of attention, word-of-mouth marketers for the author as they follow, like, and share their experiences with the content and its creator (note the excitement expressed when a "celebrity" deigns to respond to or share a follower's post).

These niche audiences – dedicated fans and consumers – have become a key marketing demographic for indie publishers and royalty publishers alike. Indie and hybrid publishers are able to develop these sources of attention because they, in effect, *are* the product. Marketing managers in royalty publishing houses have a more difficult task, as they must seek to replicate the individualized marketing with an entire stable of authors. As section 2 discusses, this has led to the standardization of social media presences for royalty authors – a standardization that produces content so bland and obviously created by marketing departments that it quite often fails, given that "online marketing strategies don't work for every author and every book. There is no easy formula that can be applied" (Thompson 2012, p. 257). In contrast, where indie and hybrid authors succeed is in the long-term development of genuine literary communities based on their work, investment in marketing beyond the six-week intense marketing blitz of royalty publishing, and development of a long-tail economic model that gives each book a much longer life to make a return on said investment (cf. ibid., p. 266; Gibson, Johnson, and Dimita 2015, p. 5).

Introduction to the Sections

When examining the effects of new technology and practices in any medium, Marshall McLuhan urges us to consider the answers to four questions: What does the new technology or practice *enhance*, *obsolesce*, *retrieve that had earlier become obsolete*, and *reverse into when pushed to extremes*? (McLuhan and McLuhan 1988; cf. Carolan and Evain 2013, p. 299). The sections that follow showcase specific examples permitting insights into these questions with regard to the evolving technology of the book, its production and distribution streams, and the environments in which author and reader connect over the foundation of common content. In particular, what happens to the role of the author in digital environments with digital tools, including epublishing, ebooks, online publishing, and social media?

This Element looks at contemporary authorship via three key authorial roles: that of the indie (or self-) publisher, the hybrid author, and the fanfiction writer. Each role is presented separately in the three sections, though it is important to note that there are significant overlaps between the three. Indie authors who achieve significant enough success to attract royalty publishers, such as Hugh Howey, often become hybrid authors. Likewise, some fanfiction writers, such as E. L. James, choose to take their writing into the commercial publishing realm, publishing either independently or through royalty publishers; some royalty-published authors keep writing fanfiction (under usernames and/or pseudonyms) simply for the pleasure of it. Nonetheless, I have pulled the roles apart here for the purposes of examination. The final "Discussion and Conclusions" section places them in analytical context with regard to McLuhan's questions, coalescing these roles into a snapshot of the digital author at this time in history, and implications for the demotic author in the future.

Through this three-sided approach, this Element frames a new era of authorship: one in which authors are not held above their readers, or apart from them. Rather, the demotic author is simply one who participates in a writing literate culture, publishing their own (fictional) writing via any number of commercial or noncommercial means. The demotic author may quest for commercial success, with an end goal of securing a royalty publishing contract once their independent activities have garnered sufficient attention capital that royalty publishers can view them as a sure bet. Once such attention capital is built, however, it conveys a significant level of power that can be wielded by hybrid authors to negotiate much better terms for themselves than previous generations of authors have been able to, thanks to the ease of digital publishing. On the other hand, many demotic authors write and publish for noncommercial aims: they write as a hobby, or to respond to a text, to "fix" it and/or add to it. They may engage in fanfiction or other noncommercial writing as a means to improve their writing to the point that they feel confident enough to transition to a commercial space; it is no coincidence that fanfiction is dominated by nonmale writers, whose culture has framed their work as less legitimate than that of their male equivalents in many artistic spheres. In short, the demotic author is one who writes and shares that writing to their audience, often regardless of extant socio-cultural norms labeling their work or their method of publication as illegitimate, amateur, or otherwise unworthy.

1 The New Digital Author

1.1 Introduction

"Everyone has a novel in them – and in most cases, that's where it should stay." Popularly attributed to the late Christopher Hitchens, this quote reflects a great deal about aspiring writers, as well as about discerning publishers and readers. A 2015 YouGov study confirms that the general British public believes they may have a novel inside them, as a whopping 60 percent of those polled indicated they would like a career as an author (librarians and academics came in second and third, respectively). Literary careers are desirable, and current technology enhances the process of becoming a published author; yet the discourse amongst publishers and academics suggests a concern for "quality," using terms like "flooding the market" and "death of humanities." Of course, as Todd Laquintano notes, those in literary power have always decried the loss of such through democratization of writing and publishing (Laquintano 2013).

The barriers to entry for new writers in the domain of fiction publishing have been lowering over the past few decades, thanks to the confluence of digital technology, marketplace affordances, and changes in public perception. If twentieth-century publishing established a top-down model, the twenty-first century has introduced a bottom-up approach that can be seen as the "democratization" of publishing, retrieving the more open nature of our previously oral culture (Ong 1982[2005]); Todd Laquintano draws on Deborah Brandt's notion of a shift from reading-based literacy to writing-based literacy when he notes that contemporary publishing is part of a "literacy practice" (2016, p. 9). His ethnographic case studies of indie publishers, both fiction and nonfiction, culminate in a concept he terms *mass authorship*, in which the book is a read-write medium (as opposed to read-only) and publishing is a literacy practice open to all writers through digital infrastructure (2010, 2013, 2016). His work is framed in Deborah Brandt's *writing-based literacy*, theorizing that while reading is still emphasized in modern education as the primary form of literacy, we have nonetheless shifted toward a writing-based literacy, thanks to digital media, social media, and writing as a dominant form of labor (Brandt 2015). Framing publishing as a literacy practice parallels Henry Jenkins's generative theory of participatory media and audiences (1992[2013], 2006a, 2007b): the digital book is mutable, participatory, and part of culture and social intercourse in a much more immediate fashion than the print book afforded.

As these barriers to entry lower, however, the concern regarding hyperabundance raises new obstacles. Putting the academic debate about quality, canon, and existential terror aside, hyperabundance creates issues of discoverability for author, publisher, and reader, in both royalty- and indie-publishing streams. Digital publishing has opened up independent and niche publishing, better enabling specialized genres and experimental forms and platforms. *Success* in digital publishing, however, depends on some of the same things successful publishing has always relied upon: a good customer base, marketing, and discoverability – which all boil down to a key element: *attention*.

Authors, like all media creators, exist in an *attention economy* (Goldhaber 1997), trading attention as a primary form of capital. Attention can convert to financial gains, as the more attention a work receives, the more likely it is to earn money from sales. Yet, as Goldhaber notes, "Money flows to attention, and much less well does attention flow to money" (1997, n.p.). Publishers have traditionally vied for reader attention through advertisements, book reviews, book covers, bestseller lists, public readings, placement in bricks-and-mortar bookstores, book clubs, and celebrity endorsements, anticipating that these wholesale pushes for attention will return to them via sales.

These traditional routes of gaining attention are part and parcel of the twentieth-century publishing machine, key factors in royalty publishers' continued success: their system is already set up to drive attention to their wares. Until recently, any new novelist who wanted to enter the romanticised index of Authorship was required to enter via that machine: to write their first novel entirely "on spec," to research agents and publishers; to craft individual query letters and submission packets for each; to send them and wait for each negative response before sending the next; to, by and large, be rejected by said machine, in favor of known authors and their recommended friends; to see "lesser" writers gain contracts because they already have attention capital in some form, whether through celebrity or infamy.

As digital technology and the might of Amazon's Kindle Direct Publishing (KDP) obsolesced these printing and distribution barriers, a new wave of writers emerged: independents, or indies. And while these indie writers and publishers can literally publish a book in seconds, there are other parts of the publishing machine that have not yet been broken down for mass utilization: the cogs and wheels that drive attention. A first-time author-publisher has neither the financial nor cultural capital to place ads in *The New York Times* or the London Underground, to request reviews in *Publishers Weekly*, or to make deals for print books to be placed in shop windows. Indie publishers have been driven to create their own forms of attention capital, and have made use of them to varying degrees of success.

This section discusses the current and emerging options for independent author–publishers to develop attention capital and convert it into financial gain. I first offer an overview of indie (or self-) publishing in order to place the current paradigm(s) in context. This is followed by an examination of online avenues to publication success: blogging, crowdfunding, and patronage. The final part of the section explores the more nebulous area of publication without expectation of (initial) monetary gain: trading free content for attention capital.

1.2 Self-Publishing Overview

Self-publishing encompasses a range of author-driven publishing practices, and its history is as long as publishing itself. As a blanket term, almost all writers (and contemporary public in general) have "self-published," whether through distribution of their own work to friends, family, and beyond; through so-called "vanity" publishing; through commission publishing; or simply through online publishing mechanisms of blogs and social media.

Self-publishing as a literary practice has been examined in great depth in other texts (cf. Bhaskar 2013; Epstein 2008; Laquintano 2016; Thompson 2005), so I won't attempt to rehash those excellent examinations. Rather, this section offers an overview of self-publishing, focusing on elements relevant to the discussion of new authors and the attention economy. These consist of commission publishing, vanity publishing, and the advent of digital publishing.

1.2.1 Self-Publishing Background

The history of publishing includes a great many self-publishers; publishing technology is a relatively recent phenomenon, and its initial uses were varying degrees of "self-publication." Notable self-published authors include Beatrix Potter, Walt Whitman, Nathaniel Hawthorne, Virginia Woolf, and Mark Twain, in addition to the more recent successes of the likes of Margaret Atwood, Hugh Howey, and Andy Weir (Bradley, Fulton and Helm 2012; Dilevko and Dali 2006). The reasons for self-publishing, then as now, were many: some authors, like Martin Luther and Benjamin Franklin, sought to distribute new ideas as far and wide and easily reproduced as possible. Others, like Charles Dodgson, simply wanted a printing of their work to gift to friends and family. Costs and copyright aside, authorial motivations in the age of print were not vastly different from authorial motivations in the age of the Internet: distribution of ideas and creativity (Ong 1982[2005]).

In addition to the pay-to-print publishing model, *commission* publishing was common in the nineteenth century, in which authors and publishers entered into a partnership of sorts, as the publishers' costs were recouped through commissions on sales, rather than upfront fees from the authors (Laquintano 2016). Even then, literary elitists lamented such a system, decrying its potential to "flood" the bookworld with too many books of substandard content, and unapproved by gatekeepers (Laquintano 2013). As vanity publishing would in the twentieth century (quite rightly, in most cases), commission publishing was largely denounced, though as we see currently, it has been renewed by digital publishing technologies.

It was largely in the twentieth-century royalty publishing era that the notion of "self-publishing" became anathema to quality and respect. Publishers grew to phenomenal cosmic powers as the gatekeepers of literary culture, though their true motivation was – as for all businesses – profit. Nonetheless, as publishers, booksellers, libraries, and reviewers amalgamated into a tangled, mutually dependent publishing machine, it became much more difficult for self-published authors to get to market. The costs of printing were still high, but publishers could offset these costs through sheer numbers, mass-producing the new paperbacks (which were also cause for literary concern of market flooding, content quality, and the like) for national and international distribution. A self-publisher had little to no opportunity to compete: they could beg shelf space from local bookshops, perhaps, and invest their own money for book tours and readings, at which they could sell a few more copies. They could establish a seminar, course, or lecture series at which they could potentially sell books. Self-published books, particularly novels, were not accepted for reviews in newspapers, *Publishers Weekly*, or listed in library catalogues.

Technological and professional barriers aside, self-publishers in the twentieth century faced significant cultural barriers to success. Aspiring writers were advised – often, by other writers – never to self-publish, because if they self-published any work, no publisher would ever touch them for "real" publishing. The so-called Yog's law emerged, which echoes still in social media streams and blogs: any publishing model in which the money does not flow *to* the author should be avoided at all costs (Laquintano 2016, p. 34). Surveys reveal that publishers and readers alike did not view self-published writers as "professional authors"; agents and publishers generally viewed self-published writers as those not good enough to make it in the royalty publishing system, and therefore unworthy of even a modicum of respect. This perspective filtered down to booksellers, reviewers, and readers.

The trials and tribulations of the so-called vanity publishers in the '70s, '80s, and '90s exacerbated these attitudes. Timothy Laquintano outlines the history of vanity publishing (2013), noting that the drive to profit from the plethora of eager writers, normally left languishing in ever-growing slush piles, is frequently viewed as predatory and unethical by publishing professionals. Not only were writers who published through these companies seen as "unprofessional hacks with unrefined texts that were not commercially viable enough to attract a publisher" (ibid., n.p.), they were viewed as naïve and pathetic for falling for these tactics. This second wave of pay-to-publish became synonymous with "self-publishing," further tarnishing the label and painting all self-published authors with this same "unprofessional hack" brush.

This prevailing attitude toward self-published authors, and even vanity presses, does not consider the many reasons people may have self-published, assuming only that they were not talented enough to make it in "real" publishing, or were too lazy to "pay dues," as it were, to get their work accepted in the royalty system. As can be seen by a simple browse of current self-publishing services, people self-publish for a variety of reasons (cf. Baverstock and Steinitz 2013b, 2013a), including local history or culture texts with limited audiences; family photo, recipe, or genealogy albums; education professionals producing learning materials; experimental projects without clear commercial avenues; and many other personal reasons that people create books outside the royalty system.

1.2.2 Self-Publishing 2007–now

As computers emerged as the next significant revolutionary technology in writing and publishing, they not only affected how writers write, but how publishers publish, readers read, and consumers purchase. All of these factors contributed to the current revolutions in writing, publishing, self-publishing, and reading practices – both technology-based and culture-based.

Publishing went digital with the word processor replacing typesetting (Baron 2009). As print-on-demand (POD) technology emerged, small presses were able to utilize this less expensive publishing technology to make smaller printing runs more feasible. Likewise, individual authors were able to make use of it to print their own texts, though they still had barriers to entry in terms of sales: bookstores and libraries would not stock these independently published texts. Digital distribution, however, was far more promising; unlike the music industry, which had to respond to online piracy and illegal file-sharing, the publishing industry never really faced significant losses through piracy, and therefore had very little motivation to enter the digital realm of publishing and distribution.

It wasn't until Amazon became enough of a juggernaut in book*selling* to enter the world of book *publishing* that the industry as a whole moved into digital publishing. Of course, digital publishing was not new: Sony had dedicated ereaders and ebookstores long before Amazon moved into the realm. The difference, however, lay with the consumer base: while tech-geeks may have sought out the Sony products as early adopters, most consumers were unaware of this option and unwilling to commit to the limited numbers of titles available (despite hundreds of thousands being available, many of these were public domain and/or outside of mainstream lists).

Once Amazon released the Kindle in 2007, simultaneously working deals with publishers to distribute digital content, as well as the KDP platform that enabled anyone at all to publish and distribute through Amazon – the "Earth's largest bookstore" – the publishing paradigm shifted. Ebooks were on the rise and would outsell print books by 2011 (Miller and Bosman 2011) (though the tables have recently turned somewhat, as Amazon's publishing deals have made some print books cheaper than ebooks [Wood 2017]). Independent publishing blossomed: from 2010 to 2015, ISBNs for self-published titles grew 375 percent, and self-publishing grew 21 percent (Bowker 2016). Subsidiary services emerged, offering editing, design, layout, and publishing to indie authors. As more ebook retailers came online, and the market expanded to tablets and mobile devices through the iBookstore and ereader apps like the Kindle app, services like LuLu.com and Smashwords emerged to help authors distribute their ebooks (and, usually, options for POD) to the various ebook sellers (though Amazon's KDP remains dominant, due to their bookselling market dominance, as well as their requirement of exclusivity for any promotional sales).

Within a few years, this surge of independently published works, along with notable success stories and cultural changes wrought by the Internet, began to challenge the perception of the self-publisher as an "unprofessional hack." For the first time, there were no demographic barriers to self-publishing (Baverstock and Steinitz 2013b), except those of digital access. Little to no knowledge of the industry was necessary; publishing, distributing, and *selling* a book was now as easy as uploading a document to a website. By 2010, "[t]he output of nontraditional titles was eight times as great as the number of mainstream published books" (Bradley, Fulton, Helm, and Pittner 2011, n.p.); this figure underestimates the number of those nontraditional titles, given that they are drawn from Bowker's numbers, which do not include books published without ISBNs, as many ebooks are. Indie-published books such as E. L. James's *Fifty Shades of Grey* (2011) and Andy Weir's *The Martian* (2011) began to populate the bestseller lists, garnering royalty agreements and film adaptations that further encouraged writers to publish their own work, whether or not they had ever attempted publication in the royalty publishing system.

This exposure assisted another significant factor legitimizing self-publishing: Internet culture. The Web 2.0 Internet culture is constructed on the basis of the consumer-producer, from social media to creative commons licensing. Publishing and creativity online often occur in stark contrast to twentieth-century mores and laws regarding copyright, ownership, art, quality, commerciality, and professionalism. Sharing on social media and consumer-generated media sites such as Flickr, YouTube, DeviantArt, and FanFiction.net is driven by an Internet gift economy (Currah 2007), a retrieval of oral storytelling sharing. Attention is part of this Internet gift economy, as it is paid in shares, likes, remixes, and attributions that indicate a level of (creative) cultural capital. The twentieth-century perception of creative work that has not been "vetted" by established professionals (agents, editors, critics) fades away online in favor of an open, sharing, creative community to the point that it is often adversarial to the established professional culture. The lack of a rubber-stamp of approval in the form of a publisher or curator may still be the sign of an amateur, but the online community is far more encouraging of the works of amateurs since many audiences are also producing and sharing their own (amateur) work. Thus more readers are more and more open to self-published, so-called amateur work thanks to the participatory, consumer-producer nature of their everyday (online) lives.

Self- (or as I will call it from this point forward, "indie") publishing has (re)established itself in the current "maker," anti-establishment, sharing, creative economy and culture. The culmination of a lack of technological barriers with the opportunity to sell (almost) directly to consumers worldwide has ushered in a new era of independent authorship and publishing. Yet, as the literary world's rhetoric has maintained almost since the invention of the printing press, this has resulted in a hyperabundance of texts (Laquintano 2016). And while Amazon and GoodReads, Apple's iBookstore, and other services are constantly producing algorithms and networks to match consumers with new products, discoverability remains the number one issue for indie publishers (Bradley et al. 2011; Bradley, Fulton and Helm 2012). Most of the market's attention remains on the remnants of the twentieth-century publishing machine: the bestseller lists (Laquintano 2016; Miller 2000; Ramdarshan Bold 2016). How then, can indie author-publishers capture enough attention to establish a bookseller foothold, to enter the bestseller lists, and to boost their "friends and family" sales into the sphere of professional authorship? The remaining parts of this section examine several ways indie publishers have pushed their heads above the surface of the flooded book market to garner enough attention to succeed.

Hugh Howey: Indie Publishing Success

Hugh Howey is now known as the first "hybrid" author, as he was the first author to negotiate a print-only contract with a major publisher (Simon & Schuster) while retaining digital rights to all his work, allowing him to continue self-publishing his ebooks while enjoying the greater capability of a publisher to market the print works worldwide and to negotiate translations and film rights (Klems 2014). Howey was able to hold out for this highly favorable contract because of the attention he had garnered with the success of his first self-published work, *Wool* (2011).

Prior to this breakout success, Howey was a fairly typical aspiring author. He had a day job, posted to writing forums, and shared work amongst his peers. Despite his initial reluctance about the traditional publishing process, he sold his first novel, *Molly Fyde and the Parsona Rescue*, to a small publisher (Wecks 2012a). Despite that positive experience, Howey felt he could do the same tasks on his own, and on a much more abbreviated time-scale; thus, he published *Wool*, a novelette of 12,000 words, through Amazon's KDP on July 30, 2011 (according to its Amazon .com publish date). The work's review history shows a handful of five-star reviews in August and September of that year, and then an explosion of positive reviews in October. Despite, or perhaps because of, its short length and low price, *Wool* entered the Kindle Bestseller list, eventually winning the Kindle Book Review's Best Indie Book of 2012 Award. Howey signed on with an agent, who aided him in negotiating his eventual hybrid deal with Simon & Schuster (ibid.).

Howey describes his success as "accidental" (Wecks 2012a, n.p.): he published *Wool* to Amazon as a stand-alone story, then continued working and writing on other projects. It was only when *Wool* began to sell thousands of copies per month, with reviewers clamoring for more, that Howey expanded what is now known as the "Silo" series into five volumes and an eventual omnibus. His success grew until, by the summer of 2012, Howey was selling 20,000–30,000 books a month, earning $150,000 monthly; he had, quite literally, achieved the writer's dream.

Few indie publishers, however, manage such serendipitous success. Most spend a great deal of time promoting themselves and their work on social media, funding their own book tours, and playing with ads and the algorithms on Amazon's Kindle Store. Many choose alternate pathways, both in terms of funding and attention; the following sections examine the current alternative pathways to indie publishing beyond simple publication through Amazon KDP.

1.3 Free for Attention

Yog's Law instructs aspiring authors to avoid entering into publishing deals in which the money does not flow toward the writer. Writers and artists are so frequently exhorted to avoid being taken advantage of that they are often reluctant to take advantage of opportunities that would benefit them in the long run. Writing forums and social media feeds are full of writers' concerns that their ideas will be stolen (disregarding the fact that ideas cannot be copyrighted and owned, and therefore cannot truly be stolen), that a publisher is the dreaded "vanity" and will thus tarnish their career, and that anyone they send their work to will steal it and publish it as their own. This side effect of the predatory practices of vanity publishing and the extremely rare instances of copyright theft has caused many writers to shy away from a beneficial business and sales tactic, that of the "loss leader." Suggesting writers offer some of their writing for free in return for the attention capital it can return, as I do in my publishing workshops, often leaves them aghast.

Nonetheless, free offerings play a significant role in the authorial attention economy. Indie publishers time specials and free deals on their Kindle books to boost them up the Kindle 100 chart, trading short-term financial gains for attention, and thus longer-term gains. Writers – known and unknown alike – share works and snippets and personal tidbits on social media and blogs, all to gain attention. Royalty publishers have discovered the benefits of offering free ebooks for a limited time, in order to boost sales (more in section 2), and of course fanfiction and art is almost entirely traded in attention, rather than sales (more in section 3). Indie authors use various methods to capture audiences' attention with the aim of eventually converting that attention to financial rewards: free ebook offers (promotions through Amazon, GoodReads, and social media), blogging/own website offerings, podcasts, and finally, Wattpad.

1.3.1 Blog/Own Site

Blogging was one of the earliest peer-to-peer sharing platforms on the Internet, predating social media by several years (Lessig 2008). A foundation element of the interactive Web 2.0, its dialectic and sharing features prefaced both social media and the open, sharing culture it would sponsor. The first blogs, or "we*b* *logs*," promulgated primarily through the LiveJournal site, and were mostly online personal journals/memoirs. Some were shared publicly online, but many were also behind log-in walls, shared only with other LiveJournalers:

a semi-public sharing with like-minded communities. The primary functions of a blog remain even now: reverse chronological organization of posts, tags or labels for topic-based grouping, subscription services such as Really Simple Syndication (RSS) or social media for update notifications, and comment and trackback features for in-place commentary and dialogue. In essence, blogging was longform social media (thus many social media platforms are often referred to as "microblogs").

As with any form of technology, artists will play and experiment with it to test its affordances and limitations for creative exploration (Benjamin 1968). Given the nature of blog technology – writing, sharing – writers easily adapted it to purposes beyond mere personal journaling. Blogging became a way to share creative writing, to form communities with other writers, and to gather readers, an audience to contribute the kind of attention writers crave: investment in their storytelling.

While most bloggers never achieve enough attention through their postings to generate actual capital, it is worth examining several instances of writers who did, in order to better understand how blogging and posting on a personal website can gather enough attention momentum to allow a writer to rise above the hyperabundant floods. Nonfiction blog/microblog success stories are far more common than fiction, particularly in the genre of humor: *Cake Wrecks* (Yates 2011), *Julie and Julia* (Powell 2005), *Hyperbole and a Half* (Brosh 2013), *Sh*t My Dad Says* (Halpern 2010), *Grumpy Cat* (Grumpy Cat 2013), along with various self-help and finance tomes. These blogs often produce stand-alone posts that are easily digested and shared, garnering nearly viral attention. High numbers of website clicks motivate publishers to offer royalty deals: these authors already have platforms to market to established audiences. Fiction, particularly long-form fiction, does not lend itself toward viral sharing: the entries are not stand-alone, they are primarily prose (lacking in imagery and multimedia), a reader can't pop in to the middle of a fiction blog and continue from there, they cannot be applied to memes or "this is so me" type social media sharing, and most are not in the genre of humor. So while blogging might seem to be a natural fit for aspiring fiction writers in terms of serial output, it doesn't grow readership in the same numbers as nonfiction and humor. So how are Andy Weir and Noelle Stevenson different from the thousands of other bloggers and writers filling the Internet with fictional narrative?

Andy Weir

Andy Weir was not a blogger; rather, he was a self-described "hobbyist" working as a computer programmer (I am Andy Weir, and I wrote "The Egg." AMA. 2013), posting his writings on his own no-frills website (Weir 2009), absolutely free. He posted a short story, "The Egg," on the site in 2009. It appeared periodically online, as readers shared and posted in forums and social media, posted cinematic adaptations on YouTube, and responded to it on blogs.[3] Weir himself reported in his AMA on the story that it had had over three million hits from 2009 to 2013, one million just since being "front-paged" on Reddit the week previous (2013).

As "The Egg" became popular enough to earn Weir an "Ask Me Anything" gig on Reddit, he was just completing his online serial *The Martian*. The novel had begun as a thought experiment: how would one survive on Mars? Though Weir had been writing and posting *The Martian* since 2009 (Garratt 2015), and had been sharing it to very positive feedback on his forum pages

---

[3] For example: Scott Craig's adaptation (www.youtube.com/watch?v=6wnShwtTkjA); The Legoman's adaptation (www.youtube.com/watch?v=pgHvGg_2Lew); Deliciae's share from StumbleUpon (https://delicium.wordpress.com/2010/07/11/a-different-perspective-you-are-everyone-and-everyone-is-you/); Shroomery's forum discussion (www.shroomery.org/forums/showflat.php/Number/13636405/fpart/all/vc/1).

(www.galactanet.com/forums/viewforum.php?f=3), he noted in his AMA that "Sometimes I'm a little sad that The Martian wasn't anywhere near as popular [as 'The Egg'], but I guess it's a niche readership. Hard sci-fi isn't for everyone" (Reddit 2013, n.p.). Despite Weir's sentiments, the novel had had fairly good success by then on Amazon, where he had released it through KDP for the minimum allowed price of $0.99; within three months "it had sold 35,000 copies and was topping Amazon's bestseller chart for science fiction" (Garratt 2015, n. p.). By 2014, Weir had an agent, a book deal with Random House, and had sold the film rights to Fox (ibid.); the 2015 film, directed by Ridley Scott and starring Matt Damon, was very successful, earning $656 million (USD) worldwide over its $108 million production budget (*The Martian (2015) – Financial Information*, no date). While "The Egg" was certainly a massive hit as a free short story, *The Martian* launched Weir into fame and fortune as a writer.

Like Hugh Howey, Andy Weir did very little to promote or market his work. He posted to his online site, and shared with like-minded friends and colleagues. He developed what he calls a "geek" following, not only sharing his work with them but using their collective intelligence for editing purposes: as he posted *The Martian* to his website, users on his forum pages gave feedback on everything from science to story structure to song choices. By the time Weir's community convinced him to publish the novel on Amazon, it had been edited and beta-tested more thoroughly than most royalty-published novels. It took time for *The Martian* juggernaut to gain steam, but the attention Weir had garnered through the viral success of "The Egg" and the free sharing of his writing on his website gave it enough ongoing momentum to smash through the publicity and discoverability barriers indie publishers typically face.

Noelle Stevenson

While Noelle Stevenson is primarily an artist, her journey from blogger to publishing success is nonetheless relevant, as comics and graphic novels are a quickly growing segment of both indie and royalty publishing. In 2010 Stevenson created a Tumblr blog for her doodles and artwork as a student at the Maryland Institute of Art. She fit right in to the Tumblr zeitgeist: young, open sexuality, quirky, visually driven, and very integrated into pop and meme culture. Tumblr exists in the middle ground between first-wave blog platforms like WordPress and Blogger, image-only streams like Instagram and SnapChat, and true microblogs like Twitter and Facebook. It supports longer-form prose work, as well as short posts leading to online comment exchange. Key to Noelle Stevenson's success, it has a "re-blogging" feature: like a Twitter retweet or a Facebook share, Tumblr bloggers can re-blog anything they see that they like, posting it to their own feeds and contributing to viral sharing.

Stevenson had garnered a sizable following to her Tumblr blog through her own work, but primarily through fan-art of blockbuster geek-hits like *Lord of the Rings* (Tolkien, 1954) and *The Avengers* (Whedon, 2012). Thanks to the popularity of the films, the humor of the drawings, and the easy shareability of Tumblr posts, the drawings became a viral hit – with some even shared on Twitter by the actors themselves (Stevenson 2012). From that point, almost everything Stevenson did gained significant attention, from her Hawkeye Initiative (http://thehawkeyeinitiative.com/) that drew awareness to the overt sexualization of female figures in comic books, to her original art and comics.

She began publishing her webcomic *Nimona* in 2012, a biweekly fantasy story about a young shapeshifter apprenticed to a questionably evil villain. The character of Nimona began as a class exercise, progressed to her senior thesis, and was picked up by HarperCollins for print publication. The graphic novel won the 2016 Eisner Award for Best Graphic Album: Reprint, and was a finalist for the 2015 National Book Award. It advanced her career, which shortly saw her winning more Eisners for her co-written comic series

Lumberjanes, as well as writing gigs on long-running series *Thor* and *Runaways* for Marvel Comics. *Nimona*'s film adaptation is slated for 2020, and *Lumberjanes* is currently in development. Stevenson's early and remarkably rapid success – all this before she was 25 years old – was driven by the attention garnered from her freely shared blog, without benefit of intentional marketing, promotion, or commercialization.

There are numerous examples of blog/own website-to-success, including a multitude of nonfiction, humor, essay, and memoir works. In pointing out these successes, it is important not to overlook the simple fact that, by and large, most of the estimated 440 million blogs (Mediakix Team 2017) and writer websites dissolve into the great sea of online writing, unnoticed. For fiction writers, even those purposely utilizing blogging platforms to promote their writing, the hyperabundance and discoverability issues are remarkably pronounced in the blogosphere, perhaps because, given its 1994 inception date, it is one of the oldest online platforms for sharing writing.

1.3.2 Podcasts

Before there was the Kindle and KDP, which renewed self-publishing for the twenty-first century, there were blogs and podcasts. Both have continued to develop and become part of the accepted media continuum, offering low entry barriers even while massive media corporations such as the BBC, FoxNews, and Slate develop corporate content. In terms of independent publishing, both have contributed significantly toward garnering attention to unknown writers often overlooked by royalty publishers.

Podcasting is often seen as an end in and of itself, though it has played significant paratextual roles in various content streams. For instance, BBC radio offers podcasts of its popular radio shows, such as Radio 4's *Woman's Hour* and *The Archers*, as well as extra content (BBC Podcasts 2018). WBEZ and This

American Life's spinoff hit *Serial*, released in 2014, pushed longform journalism podcasts into the mainstream, winning multiple media awards including a Peabody in 2015 (2014). In fiction, perhaps the most prominent podcasts are those produced by Escape Artists, beginning with EscapePod for science fiction short stories in 2005, and adding Pseudopod (horror) in 2006, PodCastle (fantasy) in 2008, and Cast of Wonders (young adult) in 2011 (2018). These podcasts offer free audio short stories in various speculative fiction genres and are able to pay their authors professional fees in a literary journal model thanks to support from donation-based subscriptions, in-podcast advertising, and patronage through Patreon (ibid.).

For indie fiction publishers, the key resource for podcasting to garner attention and potential financial capital was through Podiobooks.com (now Scribl.com). Podiobooks.com was a site on which writers could publish, usually on a serial basis, audio recordings of their books. These books were offered for free; listeners were offered the opportunity to donate an amount of their choosing through Paypal. Several authors parlayed their podcasting attention into successful publishing careers, including Scott Sigler, Nathan Lowell, and Mur Lafferty (now editor of EscapePod, a staff writer for Serial Box, and winner of several Parsec awards for her podcasting) (Gearino 2005; Hutton 2015; Newman 2007; Wecks 2012b).

The original culture of Podiobooks.com can still be seen in Scribl's welcome to Podiobooks authors, as it emphasizes that the former pay-what-you-want model has been integrated (rather than taken over) into its new "CrowdPricing Everywhere" system (which again, allows consumers to choose their pay levels). Unlike Podiobooks.com, Scribl insists on higher-quality recordings; in return, it integrates many of the elements indie publishers formerly had to do on their own: distribution through major podcasting channels like iTunes and Google Play, as well as distribution of the accompanying (and now required) ebooks. Scribl's producers clearly understand the attention capital that Podiobooks authors gained through their free offerings, as they clarify that "in addition to the paid audiobook versions on all of the audiobook outlets, a free, serialized version will appear on all the free outlets Podiobooks.com has supported" (Scribl 2018, n.p.). Scribl has turned these free podcast audiobook serials into promotional materials for the paid versions of the full-length audiobooks and ebooks, corporatizing the attention economy that indie authors like Scott Sigler pioneered.

Scott Sigler

Scott Sigler was an aspiring sci-fi novelist who thought he had made it: in 2001, he signed a deal with Time Warner to publish his first novel, *EarthCore*. Unfortunately, the events of 9/11 and the subsequent economic recession nixed the imprint set to publish the book, and the deal never came to fruition. Unable to secure another deal, Sigler turned to podcasting, recording each chapter and releasing it serially from March to September 2005. At 25,000 downloads, this was proof enough that the novel was worth printing, and Sigler secured a deal with Dragon Moon Press on these credentials (Kerley 2006).

Sigler's podcasting success inspired Evo Terra to launch PodioBooks, allowing other indie publishers to do the same with their books: record and podcast them serially at schedules and eventually price points (from free to donation to pay-per-listen) of their own choosing (Newman 2007). Authors joined the movement; Sigler continued podcasting his books, garnering significant attention capital, even as he signed with a literary agent and negotiated royalty contracts for future books (Sigler 2014). Sigler currently has "fifteen novels, six novellas and dozens of short stories" on his credits list (Sigler 2018, n.p.), with two, *Contagious* and *Alive*, appearing on *The New York Times*' bestseller lists (The New York Times

2016). He has continued his independent publishing, becoming a hybrid author in that he publishes his print work for adult audiences through royalty publishers, while independently publishing his podcasts and young adult titles through his own companies (Sigler 2018).

1.3.3 Wattpad

Wattpad launched in 2006 as a primarily mobile application that sought to be the "YouTube" of reading (Rochester 2012). Despite its rather disappointing early years, it now boasts over 60 million users, writing and reading over 400 million stories in over 50 languages; it estimates that 90 percent of its user activity is still mobile-based, spending 15 billion minutes per month on the site (Wattpad 2018). Promoting itself as a "social storytelling" platform, Wattpad invites writing of all kinds, and thus hosts fanfiction, original fiction from unknown authors, and original fiction from established authors. Its founders note that its early users were often teenage girls, though over the past decade its user base has grown and aged (Allen Lau in Rochester 2012); nonetheless, some of the most successful examples of Wattpad authors are young women, usually writing in the genres of fanfiction and/ or romance. Taran Matharu, who used Wattpad to launch his own bestselling writing career (2018), profiles six others: all women, several teenagers, who posted their novels to Wattpad and subsequently negotiated deals with Big 5 royalty publishers including Random House, HarperCollins, and Simon and Schuster (2017). These authors have successfully turned the significant attention capital gained through Wattpad's free sharing platform (1.5 billion reads for Anna Todd, 19 million for Beth Reekles, 37 million for Lilian Carmine, etc. [ibid.]) into bestselling authorial careers in royalty publishing.

Like Kickstarter, Wattpad creates a participatory environment for readers. Since authors can publish serially, and Wattpad has social functions,

"Wattpad makes the creation of the book – the writing process – a collaboration between the author and the reader" (Ramdarshan Bold 2016, p. 8). Wattpad readers can comment on the stories, share them, incorporate characters and events into their own stories, and communicate directly with the writers, engaging in a networked public sphere rather than merely receiving mass media in the form of a completed book (Benkler in Ramdarshan Bold 2016, p. 2). In this manner, they take ownership in the content, much as fan fiction authors take ownership over canonical content (Thomas 2007), even to the point that they fiercely defend the Romantic ideals of authorship and copyright (Laquintano 2016). Laquintano points out that "readers [contribute] to copyright protection by policing unauthorized distribution" (ibid., p. 150), noting that the more popular a text becomes, the more it becomes public property (p. 140). While this can have detrimental effects if a Wattpad author is seen to have "sold out," for the most part in the Wattpad community these effects are few. Readers generally seem to support their favorite authors striking publishing deals (ibid.), perhaps because they are also frequently writers who hope to achieve the same objective, and perhaps because they feel pleasure in having assisted the author in their success. This is a similar effect to the satisfaction crowdfunding backers feel in supporting a successful project, as described in the next section.

1.4 Alternative Funding and Publishing

The Internet has been a democratizing factor in many industries and communication systems. For publishing, it has given authors the ability to connect directly to readers, to establish greater connective relationships and / or build an audience. This section examines two online pathways aspiring authors have utilized to capture a potential audience's attention and convert that cultural capital into book sales: crowdfunding and patronage.

1.4.1 Crowdfunding

Novels are traditionally thought of as individual endeavors (leaving out the collaborative contributions of editors and beta readers), unlike other narrative media such as plays, film, role-playing games, or even simple oral storytelling. Online crowdfunding began with ArtistShare in 2003, and rose to mainstream popularity with the launches of IndieGoGo in 2008 and Kickstarter in 2009 (Freedman and Nutting 2015). The Kickstarter and subsequent Unbound funding platforms for publishing reverse the traditional "on spec" writing and publishing model, placing novels in the same funding model as other narrative media: raise money for a project, then complete said project (given sufficient funding).

While these platforms (with the exception of Unbound, which is exclusively for publishing projects) are perhaps better known for their funding of music, film, and start-up products, publishing is a strong division, and in fact has garnered some of crowdfunding's greatest success stories. Robin Sloan, as this section will explore, launched his first novel through Kickstarter; his subsequent royalty-published novel put him on *The New York Times* Bestseller List (Sloan 2014). Also explored in this section is *To Be or Not To Be*, the choose-your-own-adventure adaptation of *Hamlet* that broke all Kickstarter publishing records in 2012 (Hudson 2012), as well as a lesser-known but nonetheless significant project from Andrew Fitzgerald[4] in 2010

---

[4] A note about the gender and racial makeup of the case studies: the case studies were chosen because they are exemplary projects that featured heavily in news articles, and because I had first-hand experience as a backer on each. It is notable that all the case studies are projects by white, North American males. Several research studies on the demographics of Kickstarter indicate that while the platform is far more democratizing than other entrepreneurial models, white males are nonetheless favored in terms of representation and investment, though publishing is a sector that – apart from stereotypical genres like dance, fashion, and food – approaches

that demonstrates the potential for alternative funding strategies to employ alternative attention-gaining strategies in fiction.

Robin Sloan

Robin Sloan began as a blogger, partnering with fellow online journalist Matt Thompson on a wide range of current tech, geek, and event topics on *Snarkmarket* (Kimball 2012). When a co-worker and friend, Andrew Fitzgerald (discussed in a following section), successfully completed National Novel Writing Month in 2008, it inspired Sloan to return to fiction writing, something he hadn't committed much time to since his university days. He wrote and released a short story, "Mr. Penumbra's Twenty-Four Hour Bookstore," in 2009 on his own website, only promoting it through his personal social media and the *Snarkmarket* blog. Within a week, it had sold 130 Kindle copies through Amazon, and had more than ten times that number of hits on the free version on his website (Sloan 2009c). Like Andy Weir's "The Egg," it spread on social media and online forums, and garnered enough attention that when Sloan keyed into the potential of Kickstarter, his newfound fiction audience supported the effort to the tune of $13,492.00 – almost 400 percent of his initial goal of $3,500.00 (Sloan 2009b).

Again, similar to Weir as well as Stevenson, Sloan offered his readers the opportunity to be involved in the creation process. Sloan's Kickstarter proposal outlined a vague idea for a novella, and not much more; what he was selling to his backers was based on their enjoyment of "Mr. Penumbra" (which linked from the Kickstarter pitch) and the opportunity to observe and

---

equality (Marom, Robb and Sade 2013; Rhue and Clark 2016). Even in the sectors that approach or achieve equality, however, projects by men achieve far higher financial returns (Marom, Robb and Sade 2013), and so are more likely to be covered in the media, and thus discoverable.

potentially participate in the writing of the text: "The whole process is going to be really fun, too. Any amount of support gets you *behind-the-scenes access*, and I'm going to share ideas, sketches, observations, and questions as I go" (ibid., n. p., emphasis original). Toward that end, Sloan posted frequent updates as he wrote the novella, responded to questions from backers, and even used some of the excess funds to host a launch party for the book, to which all backers were invited. Depending on the amount pledged, backers could also have their name listed in the book as contributors.

Thanks to the success of his Kickstarter campaign, Sloan negotiated a contract with Farrar, Straus and Giroux, a MacMillan imprint, for his first full-length novel, *Mr. Penumbra's 24-Hour Bookstore* (2012). The novel made him a *New York Times* bestselling author, and has been published in 20 countries (Sloan 2014). Sloan gradually built attention capital through offerings first on his blog, then his own website, and finally through what was then a very new and exciting approach to selling a novel – crowdfunding – parlaying this attention into a publishing contract with a royalty publisher.

Ryan North

Unlike Robin Sloan, Ryan North turned to Kickstarter not to play with an innovative new model, but because he had already been rejected by royalty publishers (Hudson 2012). North was (and is) a web comic writer, primarily known for his online *Dinosaur Comics* (2003) and Boom Studios' *Adventure Time* series. Likely because North's comic writing career had already garnered him significant amounts of attention capital, when he launched *To Be Or Not To Be: That Is The Adventure* on Kickstarter, the choose-your-own-adventure adaptation of *Hamlet* met its $20,000 goal in less than four hours (North 2012). By the time the funding period ended, it had raised $580,905 in backing – 2,905 percent of its goal – making it the most funded publishing project ever on Kickstarter (ibid.; Hudson 2012), until Timbuktu Labs' *Good Night Stories for*

Rebel Girls bested it in 2016 (Timbuktu Labs 2016; Flood 2016). As a result, North upped the specs on the project, bringing in a team of web-cartoonists (including Noelle Stevenson) to transform the black-and-white vision to a full-color, illustrated, and printed book.

North subsequently published another Shakespearean chooseable-path adventure, *Romeo and/or Juliet*, with Riverhead Books (an imprint of Penguin Random House) in 2015, which pushed North from being a comic writer and Kickstarter success into a *New York Times* bestselling author. Riverhead Books also published a reprint of *To Be or Not To Be: That Is the Adventure* (North 2015b). While North was already a successful comic writer, he was able to use the Kickstarter platform to launch a project that royalty publishers were reluctant to take a risk on, demonstrating the benefits of crowdfunding platforms for nontraditional projects: the success or failure of a crowdfunding project allows the creator to know exactly how much attention capital *and* how much actual capital their project has generated.

Andrew Fitzgerald

Andrew Fitzgerald's *Andrew vs. The Collective* was not a wildly successful project like Sloan's, North's, or Timbuktu Labs', but like North's it is significant for a different reason: it shows how experimental works can gain commercial backing in crowdfunding publishing. Royalty publishers are notoriously risk-averse, particularly with new writers and experimental works, as their commercialization model relies on mass marketing of books rather than niche marketing. They need to sell the most books to the most people, not necessarily the *right* books to the *right* people.

Andrew Fitzgerald had already written his novel *The Collective* but needed capital in order to publish and distribute it. Instead of simply selling the novel or raising some crowdfunding merely for distribution, however, he chose to sell a participatory experience to his crowdfunders, who would in turn fund the novel. Fitzgerald proposed to write six new short stories over the course of six weeks; depending on their pledge level, backers of Fitzgerald's crowdfunding campaign could contribute suggestions to each story, which he had to incorporate. These ranged from adjectives to settings to full characters – and at the top pledge level, $100, backers could suggest anything: "No, seriously. You can give me any direction you want. Anything you can come up with" (Fitzgerald 2010, n.p.). Fitzgerald's crowdfunders were not just observers and investors in his creative journey; they were collaborative co-authors of a funded experiment in writing that previously only existed in creative writing workshops. In addition to this participatory experience, backers received updates, the short stories, copies of *The Collective*, and/or their names in the acknowledgments, depending on pledge level.

Crowdfunding publishing projects run the gamut, from new authors testing the waters, to experimental projects that couldn't find traction in the traditional royalty publishing model. Now that crowdfunding is more established, of course, many established writers and publishers, such as Timbuktu Labs' *Good Night Stories for Rebel Girls*, are turning to these platforms to fund new projects rather than relying on the risky "on spec" proposition that is the standard in royalty publishing (i.e., put all the work and effort into creating and producing the book, then wait and see if anyone wants it). Instead, crowdfunding offers these indie publishers the opportunity to see if consumers want the project first, and then to move on if it is unsuccessful.

More than that, these platforms open the space of creation beyond merely that of the novelist, inviting the crowdfunders to participate in the narrative to varying degrees. The participatory nature (Jenkins 1992[2013]) of crowdfunded publishing projects inspires reader ownership of the texts and permits greater experimentation and/or creative freedom for the authors. The crowdfunded author is released from the traditional publishing market's guessing game of commercial success, and the reader is invested emotionally as well as financially in the outcome of the project. All of the included case studies were financial successes, earning their goal funding and then some; however, the projects were even more successful in terms of reader/backer satisfaction. The projects delivered on their stated products, and the post-project reader comments are overwhelmingly positive, as readers exalt the "journey" of each project. By inviting readers into the ground floor of these creative projects, authors are both paid in advance for their work and freed from industry-imposed creative restrictions. By investing in these projects, readers gain ownership and subsequently greater pleasure in the texts that result (Zheng et al., 2017).

1.4.2 Patronage

It is worth mentioning patronage in this section, though it has been a far more successful model for established authors and thus will be discussed in more detail in section 2. Patreon.com, the most well-known patronage site, launched in 2013 in an effort to provide a better funding model for YouTube content providers (Hudson 2014). The patronage model, a type of crowdfunding, focuses on the content creator more than any one individual project. Patrons sign up to support a creator, typically through monthly contributions. In return, the content creator offers consistently updated content, content in advance of release, and often special patron-only content. It has been successfully employed primarily by video content creators, but its reach has expanded in recent years to many different types of creators, including software developers, bloggers, game developers, and authors.

Of the top twenty Writing creators on Patreon (as of January 12, 2018), only two are otherwise unknown fiction writers: M. Tefler ("Tefler") and J. McCrae ("Wildbow"). Tefler crafts erotic science fiction and has self-published two books through Amazon's KDP/Createspace services as a result of their Patreon success (Tefler 2018). McCrae writes fantasy web serials, posting updates two to three times per week. The authors' only income, thus far, is provided through Patreon along with Paypal donations through their serials' websites, but this is sufficient to permit them to write a self-described 50–60 hours per week (McCrae 2018). As of this writing, Tefler earns $2,743 per chapter, and aims to produce three chapters per month (though a review of the past three months shows they have only released two chapters per month, along with a number of other community-engaging posts), for an estimated $5,846–8,229 per month, or $70,152–98,748 per annum. McCrae earns $4,365 per month, or $52,380 per annum. These figures are a significant increase from the estimated earnings of most published authors, estimated at £4,000 per annum for UK authors (Gibson, Johnson, and Dimita 2015, p. 5) and $8,000 for US authors (Ramdarshan Bold 2016, p. 3), though 98 percent of creators on Patreon earn less than the minimum wage (Knepper 2017, n.p.). The key factor in these successes may lie in the genre (erotica, fantasy), and the high frequency and amount of content produced.

Despite these successes, advisory articles on Patreon typically note that creators without any sort of established audience may struggle on the platform; very little on the site lends itself to discovery. Clicking "Explore Creators" on the site offers links to the fourteen different media options (Video & Film, Writing, Education, etc.), six "Popular This Week" creators, and six "New and Noteworthy" creators. The media options do not break down further into genres, forms, or other categories – they merely lead to a list of the top 20 creators in that media category. A user must use the search function to find more specific creators, topics, forms, or genres. Essentially, as Booth notes, writers cannot expect strangers to stumble across their Patreon page; they need to have at least a small audience to start, and ideally an external resource for discovery that can point readers to their Patreon page (Booth 2017).

1.5 Indie-Publishing Experience

As a practice-based researcher, after having taught classes and workshops in publishing for years, I put my (mostly historical and technical knowledge) to use. I launched a sole-proprietor publishing company, dreamed up a short fiction project, and carried out the year-long process from brainstorming to book launch. While the research process of producing the book *Normal Deviation: A Weird Fiction Anthology* (Skains and Bell, 2018) was incredibly valuable, my know-how in this area was insufficient to make up for the lack of attention I had as an author and publisher. I launched two Kickstarter campaigns: the first failed, not unexpectedly. Upon the advice from a colleague who has had several successful Kickstarters, I ran the campaign again once I had all 24 authors from the collection on board, estimating that collectively, we had enough attention to fund the project. We did not – perhaps because with 24 of us sharing the load, many felt a diffused responsibility for driving attention to the project. The project had no better luck the second time around. In the end, my co-editor and I published and launched the book out of our own pockets; to date, despite our growing attention and audience, the book has yet to make a return on our investment. I would note that, unlike the other case studies presented in this section, my experience is typical for most indie publishers: a great deal of effort and work goes into *publishing* our texts (besides just writing them), but few manage to earn sufficient attention for that effort to return in capital.

1.6 Conclusion

What is quite clear from these examples is that digital media has enhanced publishing fiction in the twenty-first century significantly, thanks to technologies of production, marketing, and distribution. Platforms like PodioBooks, Kickstarter, Wattpad, and Patreon continue to emerge to fill gaps between writer and reader, often in parallel with the writer's royalty publishing activities. While democratization of writing and publishing has certainly not yet been achieved (as white males are shown to have a greater proportion of success), the opportunities to produce a wider variety of work across a broader spectrum of genres, forms, and representation have nonetheless expanded as niche audiences welcome content that caters to more specialized and specific tastes. Despite these opportunities, however, these case studies are outliers in the magnitude of their success; the great majority of crowdfunded authors and projects earn a minuscule percentage of what these examples do, just as the great majority of royalty-published writers earn a minuscule percentage of what brand-name, bestselling authors do.

Many of these success stories emerge from early adopters. Robin Sloan's project was in Kickstarter's first year; Scott Sigler put PodioBooks on the map. Andy Weir and Hugh Howey's respective successes can be explained by the attention they each received from a very small group of readers that they repaid with attention of their own; by continuing to offer content, by responding and conversing with them, by integrating their feedback, and by publishing more content. Smaller, subsequent success stories continue, and occasionally highly funded projects like *Good Night Stories for Rebel Girls* emerge (Flood 2016); by and large, however, these platforms quickly go from small innovative ponds to massive corporatized seas (e.g., Wattpad, Scribl), where discoverability becomes an issue all over again. A first-time user on Wattpad is prompted to search for "romance … paranormal … Margaret Atwood," which steers visitors not toward the fresh, but toward the known. Goldhaber (1997) notes that money cannot necessarily buy attention; it can, however, block it, at least in terms of online discoverability. Wattpad directs visitors to known authors, Patreon to those who are already successful. The bestseller lists at Amazon and *The New York Times* multiply attention; they don't create it. No one mechanism of indie publishing is the answer for very long, or for every writer.

2 The Power of the Demotic Author

2.1 Introduction

According[5] to Robert Darnton's (1989) oft-quoted life cycle of the book, author and reader are two distinct elements in the publishing cycle that do not normally interact – except by means of the book or other published object, which links them symbolically rather than materially, and more often than not expands rather than narrows the distance between sender and receiver (cf. Hillesund 2007). I would argue (with Hillesund), as Thompson and Phillips do, that the communication of fiction – or indeed any other "traditional" literary genre – is no longer a one-way street, if it ever truly was. Digital media – in particular the rise of Web 2.0 infrastructure (O'Reilly 2007) with its interactive functions and subsequent social engagement through Facebook, Twitter, blogs, and other specialized platforms – has provided opportunities for new publishing models to emerge, albeit slowly and with considerable opposition from the entrenched incumbents, royalty publishers.

Indie publishers are not the only authors who have embraced these new opportunities. While many authors established in royalty publishing continue to employ the model of distancing that evolved from nineteenth- and twentieth-century publishing practices (Laquintano 2013, 2016; Ramdarshan Bold 2016), others are using the leeway afforded to them by their success to experiment with new ways of connecting to their core audiences, and to deepen these connections. These authors are shifting the Foucaultian power dynamics between themselves, their publishers, and their readers, using their attention capital and digitally enabled "voices" to communicate with audiences rather

[5] Elements of this section appeared originally in Skains, L., 2010. The Shifting Author-Reader Dynamic: Online Novel Communities as a Bridge from Print to Digital Literature. *Convergence*, 16(1), pp. 95–111.

than participating in the established publishing hegemony's gatekeeping. The digital environment invites – even pushes – authors and publishers to abandon the stereotypical "recluse" or stand-alone author in favor of an active, engaged digital presence (Dietz 2015, pp. 200–1). Royalty publishers were and are resistant to these digital niches as a threat to their established (nearing obsolete) model, unprepared to adjust their practices of acquisition, sales, and marketing to the rapidly evolving digital environments. Yet the cycle of innovation is unending: as technology opens new niches into writing and publishing, creative innovators will continually exploit and widen those niches until they become standard, waiting for a new generation to climb above them (Bhaskar 2013, p. 172). In the publishing world, these innovators are far more often authors than established publishers.

The onus on authors and publishers to deliver content to readers is no longer centered on manufacture and distribution of a physical object; more and more it derives from attaining sufficient attention capital from consumers to (a) make them aware of the content and (b) help them invest deeply enough in it to offer money in exchange. Michael Bhaskar argues that the role of the publisher is to filter and to amplify the content; digital has converted this amplification from a physical process to a social process (2013, p. 116). Likewise, Todd Laquintano notes that "as publishing becomes absorbed into online networks as literate activity," authorship becomes sustained through interaction between author and reader (2010, p. 471). The Internet is a saturated market; as we are constantly engaged in the acts of both providing and consuming content, our attention becomes more and more diffuse across the varied media and platforms available at the touch of a fingertip. It is as easy to play a game as it is to turn a page, as simple to chat with friends across the world as it is to press play. When all reading, writing, entertainment, and interaction are presented on a level playing field, how can authors stand out amongst the crowd?

Indie publishers have a much higher hill to climb in this respect than authors who have already achieved brand-name success through print publishing. These known authors, however, are not merely treading water in their reservoirs of attention capital. In just the past decade, bestselling authors have gone from having spotty web presence at best (Skains 2010) to having a standard complement of informative websites and social media feeds. More than that, however, some authors have taken advantage of the growing power derived from reader–author interaction (Pecoskie and Hill 2015, p. 610) to implement disruptive innovations in the publishing chain, at points both obsolescing and enhancing their publishers. This section examines three overlapping areas of disruptive innovation that known authors engage in: experimentation, hybrid publishing, and social interactivity, examining how these emerging methods of connecting with readers re-invest and multiply their attention capital, often resulting in increased monetary income as well.

2.2 *Authors Who Experiment*

While it may now be standard for contemporary authors to have a clear web presence in terms of sites, blogs, and basic social media feeds, it was not always the case. Some authors have fulfilled roles as bellwethers, forging ahead in terms of innovation and experimentation, not only with form, but with publishing mechanisms and author–reader relationships. Well-known and bestselling authors, such as Stephen King and Margaret Atwood, have the wealth of their attention capital to aid them in experimentation, as Bourdieu argues only the wealthy (in some form) can (1983[1993]). Often, these are supported by their publisher, as increased author attention and cultural capital generally result in increased monetary capital through book sales.

Authors are artists; with any new technology, given the ability to do so, they will experiment (Benjamin 1968), pushing the boundaries of form and field. The author's role in the publishing industry has become isolated, diminished, and fleeting: publishers isolate authors from the "crudities" of production, marketing, and sales, per cultural norms developed via the publishing industry itself (Phillips 2014); the downturn of traditional publishing in the last few decades, whether due to decreasing reading habits (a questionable trend) or technological disruption, has led publishers to focus on celebrity and brand-name authors, to the detriment of new and mid-list authors (Ramdarshan Bold 2016); and authors who have previously had success in traditional publishing have found themselves pushed out as a result. Consider this in combination with the low royalty rates offered to even brand-name authors, and it is no surprise that many seek to turn the power of their attention capital toward making more direct connections with their readers, thus cutting out a middleman perceived to be ailing and greedy. Of course, their readers may or may not be ready for these innovations, though their wealth (both monetary and attention-based) gives them the freedom to keep experimenting.

2.2.1 Stephen King: Epublishing

Stephen King was an early adopter of epublishing and serial publishing, releasing ebooks via his own website starting in 2000 (Stapilus 2015; Thompson 2012), seven years prior to the start of the ebook boom wrought by the Kindle and iPad releases in 2007 (Phillips 2014; Thompson 2012). Thompson reports an "overwhelming response, resulting in around 400,000 downloads in the first 24 hours and 600,000 in the first two weeks" (2012, p. 314). Given the lack of uptake for ebooks at the time, and the scarcity of dedicated ereaders, mobile devices, or apps for convenient ebook display, these numbers are indeed remarkable, and demonstrate the considerable attention capital King had (and has). Nonetheless, while the experiment was relatively successful in terms of sales, and King followed up with several installments continuing his epublishing endeavors, the attempt was short-lived.

King was able to convert his enormous attention capital into monetary success through the venture (not to mention the cleverly low price point of $2.50 US) – though it is worth noting that these sales were paltry compared to those of his *Dreamcatcher* and *Black House*, released in print at approximately the same time, which reached #4 and #6, respectively, on the *Publishers Weekly* fiction bestseller list for 2001 (Bestselling Books of the Year, 1996–2007 2008) – but society was not yet prepared to afford an epublishing model (Bhaskar 2013). There was little infrastructure (ereaders, ebooksellers), and no established cultural practice for ereading. While King put the arguably top-level power of his cultural capital behind ebooks, it was insufficient to make significant inroads into establishing him and epublishing as a new epoch on its own, apart from raising awareness of the form and perhaps even gaining him more attention capital through publicity surrounding the novelty of the experiment.

2.2.2 Margaret Atwood: Serial Publishing

Margaret Atwood, while not enjoying the same massive level of attention capital as Stephen King, nonetheless has sufficient wealth to enable her to experiment in various forms of publication and digital engagement. Recently, her cultural capital has grown significantly thanks to the award-winning television adaptation of *The Handmaid's Tale* (Miller, 2017), and the miniseries *Alias Grace* (Harron, 2017). Her work has previously been adapted, and her fiction is well known (particularly *The Handmaid's Tale*, which was nominated for the Man Booker prize in 1986, and won the Arthur C. Clarke Award in 1987, and has frequently been listed in school curricula). This cultural capital gave her room to attempt serial publishing her novel *Positron: I'm Starved for You* through Byliner (via Amazon Kindle). Byliner was touted during its brief life in publishing-relevant literature as a promising model of development; like King's forays into epublishing, however, it was possibly before its time, and failed to gain any traction. It may have been inspired by the *keitai-shosetsu* (mobile fiction) and "original fiction" popular in Japan and China, respectively (Bhaskar 2013; Phillips 2014): ongoing, episodic/serial, longform fiction developed for consumption on mobile devices. This form is popular in East Asian markets, but the carefully filtered path to publishing that Byliner chose to adopt did not appeal to Western audiences; not, say, the way the open, demotic form of Wattpad has.

Wattpad, another platform Atwood has embraced, has proven much more successful than the now-defunct Byliner (or, indeed, the extant-as-of-this-writing Serial Box) precisely *because* of its demotic culture. Where Byliner's model failed despite Atwood's investment of attention capital, Wattpad's model succeeded. In some part, Atwood's attention capital helped to boost it in its early phases, but this does not entirely explain the platform's growth, given the failure of other forms Atwood espoused. Rather, Wattpad taps into cultural practices that are already undergoing significant evolution, namely the shift from reading-centered literacy to writing-centered literacy (Brandt 2015). The primary users of Wattpad, young women, are digital literates: highly active online and on social media, they are arguably more accustomed to *providing* content (and sharing, commenting on, and discussing it amongst one another) than they are to *consuming* content. By opening a space in which there is little hierarchical division between writers and readers (or none at all), Wattpad democratized fiction writing; by lending her attention capital to bring awareness to it, Atwood used her authorial and cultural power to enable thousands of other writers to participate in this new literary economy.

2.2.3 N.K. Jemisin and Seanan Macguire: Patronage

More recently, some authors (and artists in general) have been offered a platform that more efficiently converts their attention capital to monetary capital: Patreon. Patreon combines the rather old model of patronage with the new model of crowdfunding: artists, software developers, and creative producers offer content on their own terms in a subscription-like model. N. K. Jemisin, whose recent unprecedented back-to-back-to-back Hugo wins have garnered her a great deal of attention, offers her "patrons" the opportunity to subscribe to her content at different levels, depending on monthly payments. This content comes in the form of early draft work, ongoing commentary, and interaction with the author through the site. Seanan Macguire has a similar Patreon model. Both authors' account descriptions note that through Patreon, they have been able to quit their "day jobs" to write full time, a feat their success in traditional publishing (relative to the vast majority of aspiring novelists) had not afforded. They are the only two royalty-published authors listed in the top ranks of Patreon accounts (there are also two indie authors who publish solely through Patreon) as of this writing. Not only does Patreon convert these authors' royalty-publishing-derived attention capital to further monetary capital, it also amplifies it by offering their patrons illusory attention through deepened engagement with the authors' activities. Like Kickstarter backers, patrons invest more deeply *emotionally* in the artists they support, enriching the artists' attention capital through engagement, sharing, and word of mouth in addition to directly offering monetary capital.

2.2.4 Cory Doctorow and Paulo Coehlo: Self-Piracy

On the other end of the monetary capital spectrum are the "self-pirates": authors who defy logic by offering digital versions of their work for free, even now when the ebook (and paying for it) is effectively normalized. These works, offered on author websites, are both cost-free and DRM-free, qualities that publishers have long feared would devalue the book, lead to rampant piracy, and upend publishing in toto (Phillips 2014). Cory Doctorow is perhaps the best-known of these authors, a self-described anti-DRM activist. With the support of his publisher, Tor (which itself publishes all its ebooks DRM-free [Crisp, 2013]), Doctorow has consistently posted digital versions of his novels on his site, from the very first published, and invites his readers to convert them to the wide array of file types used to display ebooks (which he then posts to the site for the sake of sharing). These versions are full of supplications between chapters to buy a copy of the book to donate to a library, however, so the "free" reading experience is not entirely unencumbered.

Nonetheless, Doctorow believes this practice has enhanced his sales rather than harmed them (2006). This effect may be highly influenced by the particular audience Doctorow appeals to: tech and Internet geeks. Doctorow's works are speculative, cult-culture-driven science fiction, mired in near-future technology like 3D printing and zeitgeist worries such as loss of privacy, autonomy, and individuality. These themes resonate with media-savvy, digital innovators, and cult-culturists, many of whom are active online and subscribe to the moral norms of Internet culture (such as free sharing of information). For this audience, an author who not only "walks the walk" but *paves* the walk earns tremendous amounts of cultural capital that he can convert to attention and income through subsequent purchases, gift sales, and word of mouth.

Paulo Coehlo, unlike Doctorow, does not necessarily appeal to a particular "techy" audience. Nonetheless, he practices the same process of "self-piracy," as he calls it. Also unlike Doctorow, Coehlo did not initially have the support of his publisher, which was dismayed to find that he was offering free ebooks online (Phillips 2014, pp. 6–7), given that they were actively combating a piracy issue with his *The Alchemist*. Coehlo's response to the piracy was to offer the ebook for free, seeming to follow the logic that there's no point in stealing something that is freely available, and that whetting appetites would increase sales. As Phillips notes, he was correct, though for a somewhat different reason than Doctorow: sales of *The Alchemist* increased in foreign markets where print books had difficulty making inroads, such as Russia, as word of mouth from the "self-pirated" version spread. As a result, Coehlo embraced piracy of his work, just as Doctorow actively promotes the downloading and file conversion of his. These authors' moral alignment to the values of Internet sharing (ostensibly a "gift economy" [Currah 2007]) earns cultural capital that, via word-of-mouth advertising, results in higher revenues.

These mechanisms are only a handful of the methods that known authors choose to experiment with publishing, spending their attention capital in innovative ways to increase their monetary capital. Yet money, in most of these cases, does not seem to be the primary motivator; rather, these authors seek closer connections to their readers than is permitted through the standard royalty publishing model. King, Atwood, and Doctorow are very active on social media across a range of topics, using these platforms for personal connection as opposed to the corporatized "shilling" that infects so many other authors' (likely ghostwritten) feeds. King, at the very least, and likely Atwood, have only marginal needs to increase their financial incomes; their activity is likely driven by personal desires to connect with their audiences and peers. The difficulty to make these connections is a factor – in fact, a developed feature (Laquintano 2016) – of the royalty publishing model, which according to twentieth-century norms nurses novels like milk from the teats of its authors, shuttered in and sheltered to preserve their artistic integrity and retain the illusion of romanticised genius. The authors discussed in this section, however, have wielded the power gained through their respective attention capital, using it to disintermediate the publisher (which, in most cases, actually enriches the publishers through boosted sales). This disintermediation gives them the freedom to experiment, both in terms of creativity and publishing methods, and to follow their own artistic and/or moral agendas.

2.3 Hybrid Authors

Like the authors in the previous section, hybrid authors convert their attention capital into monetary capital, though this may or may not have anything to do with their engagement with readers on a social/personal level. Instead, hybrid authors retrieve their power from publishers in the form of digital rights: they maintain ownership of the digital copyright for their works (or negotiate for their return), while remaining contracted to the royalty publisher for their print rights (cf. Laquintano 2016, p. 88). This enables these authors to take advantage of the higher royalties offered through indie publishing (up to 70 percent through Amazon's KDP program, for example), while still benefiting from the added value of the traditional royalty publishing model, including editorial management, cover art, layout and design, printing, marketing, and distribution (Thompson 2012). The capability to choose to be a hybrid author was not always assumed, however; several authors, both royalty-published and indie-published, pioneered this "partial" disintermediation of the publisher (Bhaskar 2013, p. 65). This section will focus on the model instances of Hugh Howey, J. K. Rowling, and the mid-list authors who followed suit.

Hugh Howey began as an indie publisher (see section 1). When his *Wool* series unexpectedly took off, he was offered numerous publishing contracts. Howey turned them down, unwilling to give up the control and the more generous royalty split offered by indie publishing (Klems 2014). Howey notes that this could have been a mistake, but he didn't care: his digital sales were still very good, good enough that he considered a royalty publishing contract to be icing rather than cake. So he waited, and when Simon & Schuster was open to negotiations, letting the digital rights remain with the author,

Howey signed up to one of the first hybrid contracts in royalty publishing. He was able to churn the attention capital gained through his indie sales into a powerful new model for authors to pursue, embodying the "emerging definition of self-publishing as the process of taking personal responsibility for the management and production of content" (Baverstock and Steinitz 2013a, p. 274). Because Howey is remarkably active in the online writing community through his blog and website, he shared this power through his network.

At the extreme end of the spectrum in terms of power stands J. K. Rowling. Despite the fact that her Harry Potter books predate the rise of ebooks, and certainly the advent of hybrid publishing, Rowling nonetheless retained ownership over her digital rights (Stapilus 2015). Initially, Rowling held these rights to prevent piracy and copyright theft; as the ebook market expanded appreciably, however, she reversed her withholding position and offered the digital versions of her books on their home site, *Pottermore*, with her royalty publisher Bloomsbury earning a much reduced commission on the sales (Carolan and Evain 2013, pp. 287–8). Unlike most hybrid authors, Rowling's ebooks are not available through Amazon or other ebook retailers, only through *Pottermore*. Rowling's inarguable reign as the most influential of authors (with the most fan fiction, engagement, and sales – thus wealthiest in terms of both monetary and attention capital) permits her this control over her work, defying the epublishing adage that to deter illegitimate uses of a work, you must make it as easy to find, purchase, and download as possible. Given that *Pottermore*'s global site ranking is 7,349 (Pottermore.com Traffic, Demographics and Competitors 2018), the extra effort entailed in finding and purchasing Harry Potter ebooks is negligible.

Thanks to the efforts of authors who wield power on the upper end of the spectrum, authors in the middle – mid-listers – have gained credible power as well. As hybrid authorship has established itself, and shown that, by and large, the works are not devalued by this publishing model, mid-list authors have re-established (or simply finally enacted) their own digital rights. Mid-list authors, despite their lack of sensationalist coverage in the media as compared to new "breakout" successes, are a key component in the field of indie publishing, if overlooked. Many of the "self-publishing" successes profiled in how-to articles and texts are not new writers, but writers who have been courted, then neglected and spurned by the royalty publishing model (Gaughran 2014). Caught between the "success" of landing a publisher and the disappointment inherent in the pressurized publishing industry's focus on celebrity and bestselling authors (Ramdarshan Bold 2016, p. 16) while expecting all other authors to be much more active in the dissemination and marketing of their work (Baverstock and Steinitz 2013b, p. 211), mid-list (and debut) authors are packaging their disillusionment with the royalty system and turning it into partial, and even total, publisher disintermediation.

It is unclear in this era of paradigm shift whether any one model of publishing – royalty, indie, hybrid – will emerge as dominant and/or stable. To this point, publishers have been largely trailing behind individual and collective authorial innovators and been seen by many authors as an obsolete hindrance rather than an aid to disseminating their work to readers (Bhaskar 2013, p. 62). Indeed, the rolling snowball of power collecting for authors, as they grow more aware of their options and room to negotiate (Baverstock and Steinitz 2013b, p. 221), may never be relinquished once gained. This trend is already apparent in the numbers of royalty authors renegotiating contracts to re-establish their digital rights; as Laura Dietz points out, the authorial perception of royalty publishing has shifted away from being the holy grail, and toward a mere "credential," a sign of legitimacy and quality rather than the definition of authorship (2015, p. 209).

2.4 Social Authors

In 2010 I examined the online presence of print authors, analyzing web communities for author–reader relationships (Skains 2010). Epublishing was then rising to cultural acceptance, but online engagement between author and audience was still relatively rare; most authors, even bestselling authors, had little to no web presence. Their websites were generally maintained by the author's publisher rather than the author, with a biography, a list of publications, a schedule of events, and perhaps a contact page. Some incorporated moderately interactive elements such as an author Q&A or FAQ section. Few authors were active on social media. An update on that analysis shows cosmetic changes: almost all the authors sampled (99 drawn from the top five books on *The New York Times* Bestseller List, the *Publishers Weekly* Bestseller List, the Amazon Kindle Top 100, and *IndieBound*'s Bestseller List from weeks sampled each year from 2007 to 2018) had a standard online presence. This includes, at a minimum, the features described above in terms of an author site. The standard web presence now includes Facebook pages and Twitter feeds, though closer examination of many indicates they are maintained by publisher press offices, as the content is primarily updates and marketing for the author's latest work and activities and matches across platforms. Social media has become the norm for indie and royalty-published authors alike; *active engagement* through online communities, however, remains relatively low for most "known" authors (i.e., bestsellers/brand names).

Social authors take advantage of the interactive elements afforded by Web 2.0 infrastructures (O'Reilly 2007) to form an online community. These may include an active author blog, member forums, contests or games, and almost always now a personal engagement on social media such as Facebook or Twitter. These authors' online connection to their audience is not driven by their royalty publisher, but by their own choice to expand the author–reader dynamic beyond the connection provided by the printed text, to engage in electronic communication and dialogue, and to make use of participatory Web 2.0 tools to deepen the author–reader relationship developed from the printed text and into online digital media. By making this choice, social authors provide illusory attention to their readers, offering them a vivid sense of their deeper selves, giving them the feeling that their favorite author is paying attention (Goldhaber 1997), thus extending the authors' attention capital.

Many of the authors noted in previous sections are also social authors. Stephen King, Margaret Atwood, J. K. Rowling, Cory Doctorow – all maintain highly active Twitter feeds communicating personal information far in excess of typical press and publicity. Stephen King has 4.8 million Twitter followers, engages in political and personal tweets as well as press for his own works, and even converses with his followers, such as when he answered @hydrostaticken's question about how many books he reads per year with "About 80. So many books, so little time" (King 2018). Likewise, Margaret Atwood has 1.94 million Twitter followers, with similar types of engagement; Cory Doctorow has 437,000 Twitter followers plus the highly popular BoingBoing .net blog; J. K. Rowling has 14.4 million followers to her highly active and culturally influential Twitter feed. These revelations of personal opinions, likes, and dislikes – glimpses into the everyday lives of "celebrity" authors – form an illusory connection to their followers, which is deepened with occasional retweets and replies to individual followers.

Neil Gaiman is an author who has consistently maintained a high level of illusory attention with his readers on whatever platform is available to him. In 2010, his primary source of connection was through his daily blog, conversing with his readers about his daily activities, book signings, what he is writing about, and life in general. He later transferred these social activities first to Facebook, Tumblr, and Twitter, where he continues to maintain a highly active presence, typically posting many times a day to his 2.72 million followers. He frequently answers fan questions, and notes where their feedback has influenced him to listen to new music, read new authors, and even collaborate with other artists (Gaiman 2008). As Simone Murray notes, however, even Gaiman has found this attention economy to be a trade-off requiring frequent holidays from reader interactions in order to actually get writing done (2018, pp. 43–44).

Jasper Fforde, another bestselling author, maintains an extensive website (*Jasper Fforde Home* 2007) for his Thursday Next and Nursery Crimes series, though, like Gaiman, less so now than at the start of his publishing career. Then, Fforde hosted yearly contests encouraging readers to actively participate in his fantasy world by writing their own pieces set in the world of the novels, or participating in games or puzzles. The site, which is now largely static though still very unique to Fforde, abounded in special features, similar to DVD extras, where the author expanded on various elements of his novels. Fforde posted personal photos and news tidbits, and interacted on the member forums. In a parody of digital environments, Fforde even offered updates for each of his print works, which corrected publishing errors and misprints in each version of his novels.

Fforde certainly interacted with his readers on his own message boards, posting under his own first name ("Jasper"), and a search reveals a definite, if somewhat infrequent, presence on the reader forums during the writing of his Thursday Next series. Fforde does not maintain a regular blog as Gaiman did, though he does maintain an active presence on Twitter (and his publisher maintains a Facebook page), and he did post an assortment of personal news and photos on his original website. Fforde's site opened discourse to the reader in the form of special features that expanded his fictional worlds, contests that encouraged readers to contribute to the world of his novels, as well as the Q&A function that offered structured conversation between author and reader.

More significant to Fforde's extended relationship with his readers were the contests he himself hosted and judged in association with the Thursday Next series. Thursday Next Extreme invited readers to submit photographs of themselves in exotic locales with the author's novels. The Readers Parodies [sic] section collected items the readers themselves wrote, pieces of fanfiction that take place in the world and occasionally with the characters Fforde created. These elements, alongside the forum contributions that make their way into his published works, expanded the author–reader dynamic through discourse in online communities.

While the texts and images readers contribute do not directly alter or drive Fforde's texts, the action of creating and distributing these items to the storyworld shifts the reader partially into the role of co-author. Conversely, the process shifts the author, Fforde, into the role of reader; by reading the fanfiction submitted to his site, he becomes the recipient of text inspired by his own storyworld. His reader contributions to his writing process become clear in his third novel, *The Well of Lost Plots*, when he specifically thanks eight forum members (by their online IDs) for their contributions toward a plot element called the "Bookie Awards." One of these forum members, Twila Davis Reed (aka AllAmericanCutie), interviewed Fforde at a book signing in 2003. She notes that she asked Fforde how the forums in particular contributed to his Thursday Next series of books, and that he "related that there have been some wonderful ideas from the Fforum" (Reed 2003, n.p.). In this manner, the author–reader relationship opens, as each participant sends and receives text to be interpreted.

While Gaiman and Fforde were at one time fairly unique in their extended attention to their readers and their development of the illusory relationships that followed, newer Internet platforms are arising that offer environments not only conducive to these author–reader connections, but that require them to succeed. Kickstarter, Patreon, and Wattpad all depend entirely upon the relationship fostered through the creative act, bringing creator and audience together in a collaborative effort. For Kickstarter projects, the collaboration is primarily monetary, as creators seek crowdsourced investors; successful projects, however, require significant attention capital for the creators. Projects are far more likely to be funded if they include a video (50% vs. 30%) (O'Connell and Kurtz 2012), include personal information about the creator, and promise behind-the-scenes access and information on project progress (Benovic 2016). In fact, Kickstarter projects are far more likely to be successful if they *begin* with a solid level of attention capital, drawing on existing relationships to fund new projects. Like many other digital endeavors, Kickstarter projects suffer from a lack of discoverability (though the site is far more browseable than Patreon or Wattpad).

Patreon, similarly, requires a certain level of attention capital going in. Discoverability on the Patreon site is almost impossible, as it is not broken down any further than the major categories of Video & Film, Writing, Comics, Podcasts, and the like, and even then only lists the top 20 in each category. Rather than browsing the site for creators to support, patrons come for specific creators to support, drawn in from other connections such as social media and the creator's own site. Patreon is not necessarily a method for *creating* attention capital; rather, it is a platform for *deepening* attention capital and converting it to monetary capital. Unlike Kickstarter, Patreon does not even attempt to pretend otherwise, declining entirely to offer useful search functions to newcomers. Authors develop attention capital through their work and through social media, drawing readers in and creating a deepened author–reader relationship behind a paywall (though I note this is a rather cynical perspective). While Gaiman and Fforde did not have the technology to directly monetize their illusory attention, today's authors do, though often with severely limited success.

Wattpad, likewise, is a technology that Gaiman and Fforde (and even Andy Weir, with his own private writing forums) were too early to make use of. Unlike Kickstarter and Patreon, Wattpad does not convert attention capital to monetary capital directly; it is a free exchange of writing and discourse on that writing on an ostensibly equal playing field for all participants, from the newest newbie to Margaret Atwood (though I will note that the site owners certainly profit from ads on the site, or from Premium subscribers who want an ad-free experience). Wattpad trades initially on Deborah Brandt's writing-centered literacy (Brandt 2015). Web 2.0's affordances – social media, mobile communications – all embed our daily lives in writing. Sites like fanfiction.net and Wattpad (which does not distinguish between fanfiction and original fiction, apart from the users' own tags) expand this capability into fiction writing in an open-access, free-sharing environment true to the "California Ideology"[6] of the Internet (Bhaskar 2013, p. 54). These activities involve both writer and reader in a writing-focused literacy, focusing each on both production *and* consumption of an unfixed, fluid text (Ramdarshan Bold 2016, p. 5), creating a social dynamic that is centered directly on the fictional texts connecting them.

2.5 Conclusion

Authorship is in a liquid phase: easily transitioned to different states of being. Audiences, particularly digital literates who write as an everyday activity, are primed to experience stories in all the possible delivery systems, and to participate actively in them. By embracing online social environments that break down the barriers between author and reader, that enable the text to become a site of connection rather than hierarchical communication, social authors deepen their audiences' loyalty and attention. Social author activity aligns them with their audiences' personal interests and stances, engages them

---

[6] Based on Marshall McLuhan's theories, the California Ideology is a manifesto outlining a form of neo-liberal technodeterminism. See Barbrook and Cameron, 1995.

in discourse, increases awareness of cultural issues, and delivers an illusory attention that connects readers not only with the authors' works, but the authors themselves. This deepened attention capital can be converted to cultural and even political capital, shared with other authors and creators, and transitioned directly and indirectly to monetary capital through patronage and increased sales via brand loyalty and word of mouth (cf. Laquintano 2010; Pecoskie and Hill 2015).

Print-based culture has cultivated a distance between reader and author, as publishers curate the Romantic image of the author as a genius separate from the ordinary – or at the very least, a celebrity. In an evolving digital world, however, the notion of the text (and perhaps the publisher even more so) as a barrier between author and reader is obsolete. This deeper connection with readers not only pays dividends for these known writers, it opens the field of possibilities for all writers. The royalty publishing industry has become stale, with its precipitous state pressuring it to focus on low-risk investments with established audiences. Rather than entrenching or despairing, these authors seek opportunity in disruption (Dietz 2015, p. 210). In order to refresh the metaphorical primordial pool of publishing creativity, these authors are transcending the limits of current publishing models, opening the gates to new ways of thinking (Bhaskar 2013, p. 164) and inviting new writers coming up in a writing-centered literacy to follow them.

It is important to note that, rather than damaging royalty publishers, this shift by and large actually benefits them. The term "disintermediation" is not only unwieldy, it is ugly: it implies a cutting-out, an avoidance, a deletion. Yet all of the activities described in this section, even those in which money flows directly from consumer to writer, benefit the publisher. Publishers who, like Rowling and Bloomsbury in the early days of ebooks, fail to recognize the tremendous power of attention capital to generate revenue, instead focusing on their role as producers of physical objects, will falter in the digital era. As Bhaskar notes, "the wrongful description of identity in publishing, as makers of books rather than amplifiers of content, is at the root of the challenge; consequently, a shift in identity provides the key to its resolution" (2013, p. 167). The shortsighted view that connecting authors directly to consumers diminishes publisher capital (Phillips 2014, p. 92) puts them in opposition to authors and readers who seek to engage more deeply in new environments that support more dynamic literate activities (Laquintano 2010, p. 486). Indie publishers, as shown in section 1, as well as known authors embracing hybrid practices, demonstrate that the hierarchical dynamic between author, publisher, and reader concocted by nineteenth- and twentieth-century publishing practices is breaking down into a much more even playing field.

3 The Rising Underclass of the Fanfic Author

3.1 Introduction

The ranks of fanfiction communities have grown considerably since the era of science fiction conventions and fan 'zines in the 1960s, as the Internet has given them the ability to connect and share; the top three fanfiction-dedicated sites (Archive of Our Own, FanFiction.net, and Wattpad) boast 1,487,000, 3 million, and 65 million users respectively (Archive of Our Own 2018, Fan Fiction Demographics in 2010: Age, Sex, Country 2011; Wattpad 2016). As the demographics skew young, even schoolteachers are integrating fanfic into their curricula as methods of teaching close reading and creative writing (Garcia 2016). Yet "authorship" is not often applied to those who write fanfiction (or "fanfic"): fanfic writers, working as they do to a source text that is not their own intellectual property, do not carry a perception of authority. Copyright interpretations have kept fanfic in a subculture of hobby creativity and play, rarely permitting a writer to transition one of their texts to an authoritative position in the royalty publishing world. The values, pretentions, and misconceptions of literary gatekeepers – publishers, critics, scholars – relegated fanfic so low in their classification that even fanfic writers see themselves as unworthy of the title of "author" and the status of "published." Despite these limitations and perceptions, the form and practice persist and are growing. As this section demonstrates, writing fanfic creates deeply attentive and invested readers who not only identify with the texts they read, they take ownership of them. This confers significant cultural capital on the source text authors, but also generates *collective* attention capital for the fanfic writers responding creatively to the source text, transcending the source text and conferring a distributed authorship on the fandom.

As the field of fan studies has developed over the past three decades, various definitions of fanfic have been offered. Sheenagh Pugh offers the broadest: "writing, whether official or unofficial, paid or unpaid, which makes use of an accepted canon of characters, settings and plots generated by another writer or writers" (2005, p. 25). As this definition would include not only what we typically think of as fanfic but also adaptations, remediations, sequels, prequels, reboots, reimaginings, remakes, and a many works that incorporate intertextual references, it is too broad to be of practical use here. Abigail Derecho reflects Julia Kristeva's notion of intertextuality, Derrida's archive, and Roland Barthes' death of the author in defining fanfic as *archontic*, or texts that build on a "previously existing text," that "are not lesser than the source text, and [that] do not violate the boundaries of the source text; rather, they only add to that text's archive, becoming a part of the archive and expanding it," restricting the term to only those texts that "explicitly announce themselves as variations" (2006, p. 65). Catherine Tosenberger decries "archontic" as a passive connotation of fanfic, preferring the interactive connotation of *recursive literature* "that, whether out of preference or necessity, circulates outside of the 'official' institutional setting of commercial publishing"

(2014, p. 16). Others refer to it as *palimpsestual* (Murdock 2017; Stasi 2006), emphasizing the nonhierarchical layering of fanfic and source text. Mafalda Stasi, for her part, eschews even the term "canon," as it implies a hierarchy of legitimate/official/professional to the source text, and illegitimate/derivative/amateur to the fanfic (2006).

Outside of fan studies, the terms that are often applied to fanfic are more derogatory: derivative, unoriginal, uncreative, appropriative, amateur, dreck, and even theft. This section demonstrates that these latter appliqués are, at best, ignorant of the genre of fanfic and the efforts of its authors. I posit that fanfic forms an open-ended archive of recursive texts in a fictocritical discourse on both the source text and the culture from which the source emerged; this discourse is communicated through palimpsestual layers of both the source text's actants and those created in its fictocritical recursions, and intra-archontic and intertextual references. These elements combine to create a semiotic system that is unique to each fandom (and potentially, sub-communities of that fandom). While this definition is unwieldy, it nonetheless portrays the various qualities of fanfic that many fan studies scholars espouse, without demoting any element as derivative, low quality, or unworthy of study. In fact, in defining fanfic in such a way, I hope more writers, readers, and scholars can come to see fanfic for the rising cultural and authorial juggernaut that it is.

Condemnation has been the attitude toward fanfic for the past few decades, particularly since it evolved a new branch into media fandom. Many scholars have described its development from the television fandoms of the 1960s to the explosion of fandoms across all media (and even real people) online, including Henry Jenkins (1992[2013]), Camille Bacon-Smith (1992), Sheenagh Pugh (2005), Francesca Coppa (2006), Catherine Tosenberger (2014), and Aarthi Vadde (2017), enough that it is not necessary to repeat them here beyond a brief summary. The science fiction magazine *Amazing Stories* began to encourage fans to discuss the stories in the Letters section in the

1920s and 1930s (Vadde 2017, p. 46). Meanwhile, science fiction conventions began to spring up where fans could gather in person. Fans of TV shows like *Star Trek*, *Starsky & Hutch*, and *The Professionals* (notably often series with key male–male interpersonal relationships) discovered one another through these conventions, and started sharing their own stories based on these texts with one another. This developed through 'zines: highly dedicated fans would collect stories, compile them, and produce small publications through amateur press associations (APAs), selling them for cost to one another through mailing lists. When the Internet emerged, these fan communities found they could make use of online tools such as message boards (e.g., UseNet), blogs (e.g., LiveJournal and Tumblr), and eventually dedicated fanfic sites (e.g., fanfiction.net and archiveofourown.com [AO3]) to post their writing, read and talk about their favorite texts, and offer feedback to one another. As a result, fanfic exploded across age groups, nationalities, race, and gender; now, it is the fastest-growing form of writing (Fathallah 2017, p. 204; Pugh 2005), as demonstrated by the enormous readership on fanfic sites such as Wattpad.

Derecho traces fanfic back 400 years, to female authors responding to prominent plays and novels of their day, all the way to modern fanfic on the Internet (2006). While the latter is most important to this discussion, it is important to note that female authors have historically dominated the fanfic genre (Bacon-Smith 1992; Jenkins 1992[2013]). In the days of 'zines, these were adult women, as generally only adults had the finances and the ability to attend conventions (Tosenberger 2014, p. 8). Modern, digital fanfic writers still skew female, but much younger, as digital access is not age-restrictive and teens are a group with both the passionate investment in media texts and the free time to engage in reading and writing extensively in the fandoms. Derecho frames fanfic as "the literature of the subordinate," as women respond to media texts that "are characterized by an underrepresentation of women" (2006, p. 71). Media fandom becomes a haven for women who have been marginalized by the very texts they enjoy (Flegel and Roth 2016, p. 255). Pugh notes that fanfic writers either want more *of* their favorite texts (more backstory, more spinoffs, more story) or more *from* them: better treatment of female characters, more emotional depth from the male characters, better reflection of or commentary on socio-cultural events, etc. (2005, p. 19; Jenkins 1992[2013], p. 162). That fanfic has borne the stigma of derivative, low-quality writing from obsessive or "hysterical" women is a product of both its frequent source genres (science fiction, popular fiction, media fiction) (Coker and Benefiel 2016, p. 20) and what Judith Fathallah terms a "legitimation paradox": "the legitimation and revaluation of Other – be it racial, sexual, or gendered – is enabled and enacted through the cultural capital of the White male" (2017, pp. 9–10). Masculine-coded activities such as sports fandom, fan filmmakers using their mash-ups as Hollywood calling cards, and game modification are legitimized, while feminine-coded activities such as writing fanfic are minimized and mocked (ibid., Tosenberger 2014).

The development of fanfic online, as noted, enhanced the community and the writing practice exponentially: the Internet affords asynchronous communication, archiving, cataloguing, searching, mentoring, records of interaction and feedback, ease of distribution, and, to some extent, an equalization of status via anonymity (Campbell et al. 2016, p. 3). Fanfic is part of a network culture, "where the boundaries between authors and readers become blurred, where authors can revise and update their work at will, and where the choices made by readers are affected by the design of the Web site and the presence of menus and links" (Thomas 2010, p. 143). The move to online fanfic communities has strengthened gender segregation, as male writers stick to science fiction 'zines often aimed at male readers (whether print or online) and female writers "adopt closed online communities that replicate a form of private space" (Coker and Benefiel 2016, p. 23). Interestingly, however, it has largely been women fanfic writers who move out of these private spaces into mainstream royalty publishing, as exemplified by E. L. James and Amanda Hocking.

These transitions, however successful, have not been without controversy. The shift from fanfic writer to published author is tangled in various ethical and legitimacy questions that have hounded fanfic since the days of APAs: Is it copyright infringement? Is it profiting off others' intellectual property? Does it reflect a lack of creativity, craft, and professionalism? Is it legitimate art or merely derivative dreck? These questions arise because of perceptions about copyright that are relatively recent in human history. Prior to copyright laws, particularly twentieth-century laws, stories and characters were shared property. Shakespeare borrowed Hamlet, Juliet, Cressida, Henry, and Richard from other tales, both mythic and historical; he is not condemned as a fanfic writer. Some of these questions arise, as discussed, from the de-legitimation of the writers themselves: women working with "genre" fiction. And others, sadly, are codified by the fan communities themselves (Parish 2015; Jones 2014), as they internalize these perceptions about the legitimacy of their work and seek to protect what they do by enforcing its role as merely personal "play" (Flegel and Roth 2014).

As the following sections demonstrate, fanfic is neither uncreative nor illegitimate. Indeed, it is a form of attention so deep that it dissolves the boundary between reader and author, reader and critic, and extends "who has access to the means of cultural production and circulation" (Jenkins, Lashley, and Creech 2017, p. 1063). Far from being a subculture, fanfic is playing a significant role in contemporary storytelling; and whether fanfic writers make money from their craft or not, they are authors and may shape the future landscape of fiction.

3.2 Authorship: The Next Generation

A significant proportion of the next generation of writers is and will be digitally literate. For these writers, remix or participatory culture is not an emerging marvel to be worried over in copyright battles and pedagogical settings; it simply *is* culture. Rather than waiting for English classes, feedback from teachers, and critique in workshops to develop their writing skills, these writers are honing their craft on blogs and fan forums. As they come of age, many are entering university writing programs and finding their normal methods of creativity stifled by what they see as outdated practices and perspectives. In my observations, fanfic writers do not abandon their fannish texts as "childish things" in these environments. Instead, they use their Internet-fostered abilities to approach their different writing ventures in multiplicative ways, continuing their fanfic writing even as they adapt other texts to the formal structures of higher education.

These fanfic authors will become part of and/or highly influence the next generation of authors, and their new perspective on writing, originality, culture, and copyright will shape literature and narrative in the future. It is time to recognize their roles as authors; toward that end, this section will highlight three of the better-known authors who have already emerged from this community and pull apart the various arguments leveled against fanfic as poor quality, derivative, and lacking in cultural value.

3.2.1 Pulling to Publish

When fanfic authors, or authors who have otherwise posted their work online with free access, make their work unavailable in order to pursue royalty publishing deals, this is termed "pulling to publish." The phrase reflects the cultural attitude – shaped by copyright laws, cemented by royalty publishers, and internalized by fans – that fanfic is not "published" or "publishable" because of its intertextual (or "derivative") nature. It is seen as unethical in fanfic communities to pull to publish, as the fanfic writer is profiting not only from the intellectual property of the source author, but also from unpaid volunteers who offered feedback and editing in the fannish sharing economy, expecting perpetual free access to the work in trade[7] (Brennan and Large 2014, p. 28; cf. Flegel and Roth 2014, 2016). Nonetheless, some fanfic writers have made the transition to royalty publishing, and the mega-success of a visible few is making the practice more common. This section looks at three prominent authors who turned fan production into royalty publishing or media production success: E. L. James, Anna Todd, and Noelle Stevenson.

E.L. James's *Fifty Shades of Grey* and its sequels are now known as one of the biggest bestselling series in the world. The origins of the books, as is also fairly well known, are in fanfic and self-publishing: James wrote and posted them (originally titled *Master of the Universe*) as fanfic in the *Twilight* archontic text (source author: Stephanie Meyer), utilizing a great deal of commentary, feedback, and beta editing from that fan community (Brennan and Large 2014). James chose to self-publish through The Writers' Coffee Shop (which specialized in publishing pull-to-publish fanfic via POD), drawing on the attention capital she had developed through the fanfic. Indeed, this attention capital directly led to her royalty publishing agreement, as it was a reader-directed launch party for the third novel in the self-published series that included a Vintage Anchor executive who picked up the series (Pecoskie and Hill 2015, p. 695). While attention capital drove her success, it was not entirely positive: the fan community perceived James' "filing off the serial numbers" (deleting identifiable references to its source text) and pulling to publish as a betrayal of the community and an exploitation of community efforts to improve the work through feedback.

---

[7] I would note that feedback and editing exchanges are also typical for *most* creative writers, not just fanfiction, and that, outside of professional services, no one in the writing community expects payment or forever-free access to these works as trade for their activities. Rather, these activities are traded like-for-like.

Anna Todd enjoyed a more direct route from fanfic to royalty publishing, via her enormous Wattpad popularity "posting" (Wattpad, in a reflection of fanfic norms, does not refer to these posts as "publishing") real-person fanfic based on the band One Direction. As the number-one author on the platform by far, Todd had garnered significant enough attention capital for royalty publisher Simon & Schuster to offer her a contract (Reid 2014). Unlike James, Todd negotiated a deal to allow her Wattpad work to remain. Nonetheless, Todd's move to royalty publishing received backlash from various directions (Alter, 2017); as with James, many in the community viewed it as profiting off her readers (Ramdarshan Bold 2016).

In contrast to the community backlash both James and Todd suffered, Noelle Stevenson launched herself into royalty authorship and media production via online fan production with little to no negative response from her community. Stevenson's fan work, unlike James' and Todd's, was not only transformative but *remediating*: she responded to Marvel's Avengers films and comics (among other media properties) with drawings and comics, rather than prose fictions. Further, her webcomic *Nimona* was not a fannish text responding to any particular source text, though its style and narrative were clearly influenced and developed by the fannish texts she had previously produced, shared, and discussed on her Tumblr blog. Stevenson pulled *Nimona* to publish with HarperCollins, making inaccessible the thousands of reader comments and fannish contributions of their own that had been posted to the online webcomic. *Nimona* went on to earn nominations for a 2015 Eisner Award and the 2015 National Book Award, winning a 2015 Cyblis Award (Alverson 2016; Asselin 2015; Dwyer 2015; Robinson 2015), and Stevenson shot to prominence at a remarkably young age as a graphic novelist. At no point was she denigrated for her early (or ongoing) fan art. Rachel Parish notes that the remediation of the source texts to art rather than prose for these fan producers "alleviates some of the concerns of 'theft'" (Parish 2015, p. 112), and Bethan Jones notes that even selling fan art online (such as through Etsy and RedBubble) is seen as okay and ethical by fan communities (Jones 2014).

The receipt of Stevenson's work in comparison to that of James and even Todd (quality judgments notwithstanding) demonstrates the conflicting perceptions of creativity, authorship, originality, and legitimacy surrounding artistic practices inspired by and responding to texts that are currently under copyright. After all, numerous well-received literary texts can easily be classified as fanfic, even in the most restrictive of definitions: Tom Stoppard's *Rosencrantz & Guildenstern Are Dead*, Jean Rhys's *Wide Sargasso Sea*, Gregory Maguire's *Wicked*, Cory Doctorow's *Little Brother*, Neil Gaiman's *The Graveyard Book*, Alice Randall's *The Wind Done Gone*, Nancy Rawles's *My Jim*, Sena Jeter Naslund's *Ahab's Wife*, and more. These works are less derivative of their source texts than many fanfics – and in many ways are far more so, as they haven't even had serial numbers filed off. The following section examines the arguments against legitimation of fan texts in order to suss out the source of these conflicting perceptions.

3.2.2 De-mystifying Fanfic

What Lessig calls "Read/Write" culture (2008), Barthes terms "writerly" (1975), and Jenkins defines as "participatory" (2006a), Walter Ong denotes as a mediated return to oral culture (Ong 1982[2005]). While the twentieth-century model of mass media communication and copyright ownership seems natural to extant generations, it is nonetheless a rather recent and strange imposition on human narrative traditions. Digital media's retrieval of folksonomic sharing, remediating, remixing, responding, and recreating harkens to the oral storytelling days of hearing, memorizing, reshaping, and retelling that originated all narrative, forming a secondary orality as print culture's written elements merge with oral sharing (ibid.). Thus Jenkins argues that in the current convergence, participatory culture is "reaffirming the right of every-day people to actively contribute to their culture" (2006a, p. 136). While the print-zine culture of twentieth-century fanfic bought entirely into print culture's hierarchy between author, text, and reader/fan, the twenty-first-century online fanfic culture is re-mythologizing the word, bringing literature back to Ong's orality. Perceptions of fanfic as lesser and unworthy of attention are mired in what could be argued is an antiquated and temporary fugue borne of twentieth-century insecurities. This section examines these perceptions, one by one, noting their likely origins, and offers alternative perspectives that legitimate this culturally relevant and rapidly expanding form of creative authorship.

Perception 1: Fanfic is poor-quality writing. Some of it is. As with any creative realm, there will be a great deal that is poor, much that is mediocre, and a small proportion that is excellent. There are multiple factors that play into this perception of fanfic. Unlike amateur writing that is submitted to magazines and royalty publishers, fanfic is *public*. Not only can everyone see the very good works, they can also see the very bad works, and since fanfic demographics for online communities skew *young*, that means that many of these authors are writing for the first time. Not many "seasoned" writers would want the world to see our adolescent efforts; it is unfair to judge fanfics simply because all efforts are visible. Further, cultural "taste is always in crisis": we tend to assume that because we personally – or the gatekeepers in terms of publishers, awards committees, and education policy-makers – have a particular taste, it is therefore natural and universal (Jenkins 2006a, p. 136). The contrast between books on the bestsellers lists, books on the awards lists, and texts that fans devote considerable attention to show that no taste is universal, and there is room for all.

Fanfic, as well, has a unique quality that often closes it off to outsiders. It is written not for wide or mainstream audiences, but for other fans. Fanfic exists as entries into an ongoing fictocritical discourse with the source text and those that respond to it; by its nature it is intertextual, self-referential, and builds its own unique semiotic system through these archontic references. It cannot be separated from its palimpsest (Flegel and Roth 2014, p. 1092), and thus its actual readers correspond with its ideal readers: other very active readers (Landow 2006), fans, and fanfic writers (Coker and Benefiel 2016; Pugh 2005). Readers not within this group are unlikely to grasp its purposes, complexities, references, and depths, and are thus more likely to perceive it, unjustly, as poor quality. And, Cornel Sandvoss notes, the field of literary studies has historically emphasized the creative text as unique and stand-alone (2007[2014]), the product of "original genius" or "divine inspiration." As fanfic (necessarily) places texts in context to their source and to one another, this notion of distributed authorship seems antithetic to twentieth-century conceptions of creativity and authorship, placing fanfic outside accepted realms of literature.

Perception 2: Fanfic is derivative/not creative. This perception is not new, and it is also applied to remixed art such as video mashups: "why can't these artists simply apply their talents to 'original' art?" As noted above, the meaning in these works *comes from* the intertextual referencing and juxtapositioning of the source material (Lessig 2008, p. 99). Fanfic writers are not rehashing or reproducing their source texts; they are springboarding off them to rework, respond to, repair, eroticize, and/or add new creative texts (Jenkins 1992[2013], p. 162). Fanfic writing offers avenues to expand the source text, recontextualize it, refocus it, shift genres, adjust representation, intensify subtextual emotional content, and even personalize to the writer's identity (ibid.; Tosenberger 2014). As Pugh notes, fanfic is created on two premises: the source creator cannot know everything there is to know about the characters and storyworld, and said actants and universe can *transcend* their source texts (2005).

This transcendence is a far more appropriate descriptor for fanfic than "derivative," "uncreative," or "appropriative." Drawing on Deleuze, Derecho argues that repetition of something need not be derivative or simple duplication – it can include differences that make it new and unique, and even a commentary on the first instance, making actual the wealth of potentialities present in the source (2006; Goodman 2015). Further, without the limitations inherent in creating a source text, such as internal consistency, chronological logic, length, and the like, fanfic is permitted a creative freedom with the property that the source author cannot enjoy (Tushnet 2017, p. 85). This creativity is apparent in fanfics that "fill in gaps" in storylines and character relationships, that delve deeper into emotional connections that many media productions do not have time or budget to explore, that cross over into different universes and fandoms, and that respond through creative writing to cultural issues and representation – works that do not so much recreate their source materials as transcend them.

Perception 3: Fanfic does not develop the writer. This perception is perhaps a conclusion drawn from the previous two: if the fanfic that is out there is derivative and of poor quality, then obviously the practice of writing fanfic does not produce good writers. This is a specious conclusion at best. Fanfic communities have historically engaged in improvement of craft. The print-zine era saw 'zine editors fulfilling editorial roles: calling for submissions, outlining author guidelines, selecting works, feeding back to authors, and copyediting (though some did less, others did more); Jenkins notes fanfic as an important training ground for professional editors and writers (1992[2013], p. 47). Upon shifting to online communities, the traditional writer-editor hierarchy (like the author-reader hierarchy) equalizes into a system of distributed mentorship (Campbell et al. 2016; Evans et al. 2017) as fanfic writers employ "beta-readers" to help develop and proofread their work before posting online, and reader feedback in the form of comments on each posting (Black 2009;

Karpovich 2006; Lammers 2016; Thomas 2010). Jayne C. Lammers, in encouraging educators to make use of fanfic writing in the classroom, notes that fanfic sites strongly resemble online writing workshops (2016, p. 9). In my own experience, more and more of the writers entering the program in which I teach are coming from fanfic backgrounds; if as a whole they are not *better* than their peers who do not engage in fanfic, at the very least they are not any *worse*.

Of course, not all fanfic writers, like writers in general, make extensive use of this distributed mentorship system. The community certainly allows fanfic writers to opt out of critical feedback, and simply bask in whatever accolades they may receive – a practice that is welcoming and encouraging, but doesn't necessary lead to improvements in writing quality (Flegel and Roth 2016, p. 257). Some eschew beta-readers *because* they've already been through writing programs and feel superior to other fanfic writers (having internalized the literary studies field's perceptions of fanfic) (Karpovich 2006). Some fanfic writers don't care that they are not improving; their goal is not to be better writers, but simply to engage with other fans and have fun with their work (Pugh 2005). Just as not all weekend athletes aspire to become professionals, not all writers aspire to become royalty-published authors. The expectation that if one is writing, one must want to become accepted by the literary hegemony ignores the many and varied motivations that people have to write and leads to specious value judgments as a result.

Perception 4: Fanfic trades in lesser genres. These genres include science fiction/fantasy (SFF), romance, and eroticism; the former is the realm of "popular" and often derivative genre fiction, as decried by presumed gate-keepers of literary quality, while the latter two are in the traditional realm of women's writing (and also part of the maligned "popular" work). In terms of SFF, twentieth-century fanfic originates in this genre, with the SFF magazine *Amazing Stories* prompting fan discourse in its letters pages, SFF conventions bringing fans together, and *Star Trek* serving as a popular first fandom for recursive writing (Vadde 2017, p. 46). The more popular a source text was, the more likely fans were to find other fans, and thus spark up a 'zine. The age of the Internet rendered this criterion moot, as it enables fans of even the most obscure texts to find one another. Nonetheless, the speculative nature of writing fanfic is complementary to the speculative nature of SFF: both ask "what if?", filling in gaps, looking at events from different perspectives, and pushing the boundaries of both actual and fictional universes (Pugh 2005). Fanfic is thus colored by the perception of the SFF genre as of lower merit and cultural status (Jenkins 1992[2013], p. 53), which neither deserves.

Fanfic, naturally, is not restricted to the SFF genre; its association with women writers and female-dominated genres, however, similarly connotes its perception as "lesser." Jenkins posits that male writers accept an authorial authority and are conditioned to take on a mantle of authority themselves when they construct new texts, while women are more likely to see themselves "as engaged in a 'conversation' within which they [can] participate as active contributors" (1992[2013], p. 108). In combination with the fact that women had and continue to have fewer opportunities at "legitimate" publication, that fanfic gives them a shielded and encouraging community, and that this practice allows for a fictocritical response to their lack of representation in and behind texts, their prominent numbers in fanfic authorship are understandable. In return for this activity, however, insidious gender bias has infused the perception of fanfic as being subordinate, illegitimate, and even weak: male media fans are stereotyped as homosocial and insular (in contrast with the heteronormativity of sports fandom), female media fans as obsessive and psychotic (Stanfill 2018). Because the act of writing fanfic is not perceived to be an activity attributable to white, heteronormative males, it suffers Fathallah's "legitimation paradox": similar activities perceived to be the realm of white, heteronormative males (e.g., mashups, game mods) are legitimate, whereas female-driven activities are not (Fathallah 2017).

Finally, there is a failure to recognize fanfic as a legitimate genre in and of itself. As noted above, fanfic is archontic, recursive, and intertextual, forming semiotic systems unique to each fandom; it is inseparable from its source text; and it is written for a specific audience of similarly knowledgable and very active readers. It incorporates genre forms that are very short ("drabbles": exactly 100 words), very long (serial novels), unstructured (character studies), inconsistent with the source and/or other fan texts, ergodic (requiring nontrivial effort [Aarseth 1997], as fanfic authors challenge themselves to be as succinct within their fandom's semiotic system as possible [Pugh 2005]), and otherwise playful and experimental – all within the same archontic text. Not only are these elements of fanfic outside the royalty publishing realm and thus mainstream awareness, they are defining conventions of the fanfic genre, rendering it both un-royalty publishable and transcendent.

Perception 5: Fanfic is unethical. The primary argument that fanfic is unethical is that it is "stealing" another's intellectual property. Various authors, including Anne Rice (2008) and George R. R. Martin (2010), have described it as such, asserting their (perceived) ownership over their characters, and noting that they do not want to see what other authors would do to them. Pugh points out that this ethical line is only seen to be crossed because the authors of these source texts are still living to witness them; similar treatment of texts that are out of copyright have no such ethical taint (2005). In terms of copyright law, where fanfic lies in terms of fair use versus infringement has yet to be determined by the courts (De Kosnik 2009), and in fact the twenty-first-century legal landscape is more favorable to the categorization of fanfic as "transformative" (and thus, fair use), protecting it against accusations of infringement (Tushnet 2017, p. 78). Financially speaking, fanfic is more likely to bring financial reward *into* the source text as it builds attention capital that increases its market; fanfic is thus a remarkable (and free) tool for marketing and sales promotion (De Kosnik 2009; Lessig 2008; Knobel 2017; Pugh 2005). Numerous authors and media properties have already figured this out, including Gaiman (2004), Doctorow (2007), J. K. Rowling (Harry Potter: Meet J. K. Rowling, 2000), and even Ursula Le Guin (no date), encouraging (or at least tolerating) fanfic based on their source texts. Further, whether for its own good or ill, the fanfic community reverses into copyright culture, as seen in its policing of plagiarism, its taboo on pulling to publish, and its "[philosophical opposition] to hierarchy, property, and the dominance of one variant of a series over another variant" (Derecho 2006, p. 77).

Media and publishing industries, recognizing fanfic's attention capital as ripe with potential for commercialization, have already endeavoured to transition it to commercial markets, with very little success – which is probably to the good of the fanfic community, given what Vadde describes as "the detrimental potential of Web 2.0 companies to exploit amateurs and appropriate their creativity for private enterprise" (2017, p. 28). FanLib (now defunct) and KindleWorlds (still limping on) are both corporate, top-down attempts to monetize the popularity and abundance of fanfic – both without understanding the fundamental qualities of fanfic that make it so. Amazon's KindleWorlds has licensed specific media properties (*Gossip Girl*, *The Vampire Diaries*, and *Pretty Little Liars*, among other lesser known texts) for fanfic writers to contribute to; it does so, however, without consideration of the generic conventions or creative freedom inherent in fanfic, imposing restrictions on timelines, length, form, and content (Coker and Benefiel 2016, p. 24). These limitations, offered for a cost to readers, produced (a small amount of) work that could not compete with the wealth of fanfic available for free in online communities (ibid.). Other players have entered the scene. Wattpad, free for writers and readers, is nonetheless attempting to convert the enormous attention capital generated by the fanfic on the platform into financial capital via premium services and brand-name authors; AO3 shows monetary potential in its internal funding drives (Hellekson 2015, p. 130); and individual authors such as E. L. James and Anna Todd have shown that the transition to royalty publishing is possible. The key to these efforts' success or failure lies in their deference to the core values and conventions of fanfic and the fanfic community; from these communities' perspectives, transitioning from gift economy to commerce from without is far more unethically exploitative than the entire practice of writing fanfic is to begin with.

3.3 Fan Attention

Fanfic writers, like many citizens of the Internet, are part of what Lessig terms a "Read/Write" (RW) culture: they "read" their culture in books, games, films, and TV shows, and they add to that culture by reimagining (or "remixing") it in different ways (2008, p. 46). In order to read-write their culture, fanfic authors fulfill three key roles: those of reader, critic, and author.

As readers, fans are never casual; rather, they are "very active readers" (Landow 2006). They accept the source text, and what's more, they are passionate about it. Re-reading the source text is central to the fanfic writer's aesthetic pleasure in it (Jenkins 1992[2013], p. 69) – and while re-reading may be antithetic to the culture of capitalism and commercialism that urges audiences to finish a text and move on to (purchase) the next thing (Barthes 1975), it is part of the deep attention that fans give to a text in order to interpret, analyze, and take ownership over the source materials. Online communities afford the fan audience the opportunity to share and grow its knowledge of the source text until it has as "thorough a knowledge of its particular shared canon as a Bible-reading or classically educated audience once did" (Pugh 2005, p. 219). They create archives of information and knowledge through wikis, discussion forums, and ongoing interaction – a sophisticated yet informal process that

mirrors the collection, sharing, and gatekeeping of scholarly knowledge (Price and Robinson 2017, p. 655). This deep attention, leading to discourse and creative response, is a mechanism for establishing an audience (Phillips 2014); certainly, the increase in sequels, prequels, reboots, and remakes, and even the resurrection of various media properties in recent years demonstrate the recognition of this highly invested audience from commercial media producers.

The comparison of fan knowledge to the level of scholarship is not unwarranted. Jenkins notes that fans' repeated viewings allow them to see characters and stories as simultaneously "real" and "constructed," permitting both suspension of disbelief and ironic distance (1992[2013], p. 66). This strategy is not unlike the position of the academic critic – after all, many of us choose texts to study because we are passionate about them, and in order to keep them "safe" from the often negative effects of close reading and deconstructive analysis, we enjoy them on one level even as we dissect them on another (at least, that is true for me). Fans' discussion of their source texts bears the hallmarks of close readings and interpretation associated with such literary analysis (Thomas 2010, p. 152); these interactions form a multitude of understandings, much as scholarly discourse does in a more formal capacity, from which characters and stories can grow and change (Kaplan 2006, p. 137). If, from a fan's perspective, a text's stories and characters consist of both the source materials and the palimpsestual fanfics that overlay it, if its power and meaning are constructed by the fan as reader, critic, and eventually co-author, then, as Sandvoss notes, the author may not be dead – only distributed (2007[2014], p. 69).

For fanfic writers are indeed authors, in the sense of both Foucault and Barthes: they are asserting power over the source texts by challenging the ideas and representations presented (Garcia 2016, p. 354), and they are filtering culture through the texts they contribute. Karen Hellekson and Katrina Busse define the fannish text as Barthes' *writerly* text, one open to shared authorship, discourse, and play (Hellekson and Busse 2006, p. 6). As creative writers, we are taught the importance of reading: knowing our genre, our competition, our history, seeking an elusive "originality." We cut our teeth on "canonical" authors and are told to strive to write as they do (of course, always with our own "original" take). Yet we are also taught the necessity of writing to an audience: speaking to cultural issues, aligning with (or artistically questioning) conventions, and even aiming for a target market. Many respected authors are both writers and scholars, writers and teachers (ignoring the financial necessities of these arrangements). We acknowledge that our deep attention to texts and our analytical understanding of structures and techniques enhance our capabilities as writers. If, as Barthes posits, we are culture grinders, chewing up our knowledge, experience, and the texts we read and spitting them out again as "original" work, are we not all fanfic writers?[8] The fanfic author's process is little different from this, save that its intertextuality is explicit, and drawn from works still under copyright (Pugh 2005). It is this intertextuality and the juxtapositions between source and other cultural materials that provide such pleasure to the fanfic author (Jenkins 1992[2013], p. 37). The extraordinary cultural knowledge and artistic craft required to create works that resonate with the target audience – similarly knowledgeable expert and very active readers – stand in stark contrast to the accusations of fanfic as derivative,

---

[8] A related anecdote: upon reflecting on this question, I realized that both my first attempts at writing (as described in the opening paragraph of this Element's introduction) and my first published short story were fanfiction texts. The first was a transformation of Judy Blume's Superfudge series into my own life, and the second was a projection of Tennessee Williams' *A Streetcar Named Desire* 30 years on. Despite my formal "literary" creative writing training, which eschewed fanfic as derivative and childish, I nonetheless unknowingly wrote many pieces that could be considered fanfic throughout my career, without ever being accused of such.

lacking creativity, and only practiced by those who can't make it as "real" authors.

In becoming authors in and of themselves, fanfic writers take ownership of the source texts, or at least the actants, settings, and events within them. In contributing new palimpsestual layers to the source text, fanfic writers invest a great deal of attention (and usually money as well), developing a sense of ownership in writing, sharing, and discussing with others, and framing the archontic text in their own terms (Jenkins 1992[2013], p. xxi). While fans are often portrayed in media as slavish, pathetic, and sycophantic, in actuality they convey a great deal of strength and mastery in the discourse and texts they produce. A fanfic writer must provide their own authorization to actively participate in shaping a text (Coker and Benefiel 2016, p. 26); they must feel free to disregard the source author's authority (Goodman 2015, p. 668) and enter into discourse with them either directly through social media, or indirectly through the fictocritical discourse of fanfic. Fanfic writers, in shaping their responses to the source author and/or culture, give themselves the authority to alter and play with the source text; this sense of ownership extends to feelings of indignation should the source author "betray" a continuing text's characterizations, storyworld, or "canonical" conventions (ibid., p. 667). It also extends to community policing against plagiarism (Tushnet 2017, p. 82) and the community taboo against "filing off the serial numbers," which is seen as stealing from the source author and the fan community of beta readers and commenters alike (Jones 2014; Parish 2015).

3.4 Conclusion

Despite the lack of remuneration for their efforts (and sometimes because of it), and despite the negative perception of their work's legitimacy and quality, fanfic writers are nonetheless a force to be reckoned with, placing "transformative pressure on august institutions of literature, from the publishing house to professional authorship to reviewing culture" (Vadde 2017, p. 27). These pressures are enabled by networked technologies connecting vast numbers of fans together in a public socio-cultural space that affords them considerable collective power. Using that power, fanfic writers are challenging dominant cultural hierarchies, including that of the author-text-reader, as well as those of the still-dominant patriarchy. In so doing, they are establishing a discourse outside of mainstream media that nonetheless has power to direct it.

The element still holding fanfic back from reaching its potential as a true form of literary creativity and a creative writing genre in and of itself is its internalization of and reversal into twentieth-century perceptions of its illegitimacy. Fanfic culture continues to approach its own texts apologetically, denouncing ownership in the header of each text and mobbishly excoriating any of their number who dare to "file the serial numbers off" and seek payment for their own creativity (even the phrase "filing the serial numbers off" references theft). This attitude persists despite the unprecedented success of E. L. James and others from their community; the negative self-perception of fanfic legitimacy is so deeply ingrained that they see these successes as betrayals, rather than accomplishments worthy of lauding.

Unlike royalty-published, indie-published, or hybrid authors, fanfic authors are ushering in a new era of prose fiction: one that is open-ended, palimpsestual, intra- and intertextual, inviting to new contributions, shaped around community and discourse, with room for multiplicative forms of creativity, play, and experimentation. Despite the arguments in this section, fanfic writers may not need external validation for the legitimacy of their work: given their numbers, their passion, and their youth, they may simply shift cultural reading habits to their new realm, rather than attempting to fit into the old one.

Discussion and Conclusions

The demotic author is not defined by the size of their name in relation to the title of their book; while they may rise to bestseller success, they also may remain in the oft-denoted realm of "amateur," sharing their writing in a gift economy. The demotic author is not defined by their form, their genre, the number of copies sold, or their ability to obtain a royalty publishing contract; rather, they are authors because they connect to readers, regardless of platform, awards, medium, or method of distribution. Demotic authors define themselves as writers simply by writing *and sharing* their work, finding the best technology and path to readership that suits their own personal goals, regardless of their culture's or their own perceptions of their work's "legitimacy" and/or quality.

For new novelists in an era of risk-averse royalty publishers, this means embracing alternative mechanisms for publishing, disintermediating royalty publishers. Previous success stories, such as Hugh Howey, Andy Weir, Amanda Hocking, and Robin Sloan, light the way for these writers as they examine their options. On one hand is a years-long, dim trudge through queries, rejections, and many choices and changes regarding their work that disenfranchises them to varying degrees and rewards them with a pittance in terms of royalties, if they ever achieve "success" in the form of publication at all. On the other is a quick and easy route to publication that affords instant gratification, complete control, significantly higher royalty percentages, and a more direct connection to readers, without nullifying the usually more lucrative path (via advances, volume sales, and film rights sales) to royalty publishing should their work prove popular.

As the figures indicate, more writers are becoming published authors thanks to these innovations, yet the returns on average are diminishing: strapped royalty publishers offer fewer and lower advances, newly emerging markets become flooded and works suffer decreased discoverability, and many platforms emerge in an Internet gift economy that enculturates writers to disavow their intellectual property rights and readers to expect works for free. The writers who have achieved key success through indie publishing are those whose works, whether by chance or by design (usually by chance), reach key audience members. For E. L. James, it was a reader who hosted a book launch party that a royalty publisher attended; for Andy Weir and Robin Sloan, it was science and tech "geeks" who embraced their content and promoted it via word of mouth; for Noelle Stevenson, it was the Tumblr community that churned her amusing sketches into fan memes. It is crucial to recognize that these authors are exceptions rather than norms: most indie authors earn somewhere around $500 (Camacho 2013), and even that is skewed upward by high earners like the ones featured in this Element.

Nonetheless, these writers achieve authorship through their publication and connection to their audience, regardless of monetary compensation or the size of their readership. This niche readership – large or small – exerts a level of ownership over the text, taking pride in "discovering" it and its author, sharing it excitedly with others, and recommending it on social media and in consumer reviews. These communities form regardless of the author's location, gender, age, regardless of the novel's genre, length, and even the quality of the writing. Not all readers, after all, read for aesthetics, cognitive challenge, or socio-cultural or personal reflection – aspects that can be attributed to "literary" texts. Most read for entertainment, and what a reader finds entertaining is as varied as people are. As more texts become available, more readers are able to connect with works and authors in their desired niche, establishing authors, genres, and niches that never existed before. In this paradigm, the only bad writing is that which fails to meet its particular audience's needs. Not only does indie publishing democratize the practice of writing and publishing, it also democratizes cultural taste.

Author-reader communities, connecting through these niche texts and meeting the needs and desires of both writer and audience, generate a key commodity in contemporary culture: attention. Established authors, whose names have developed into brands, maintain extended attention capital through their work. They emerge in and are buoyed by the royalty publishing structure, but recognize the opportunities presented by newer media. Rather than hiding behind the romanticised notion of the author as divinely inspired creative genius eschewing any connection to the reader save that of the text, these authors establish online presences that afford multiplication of their attention capital. By interacting online through social media, these authors offer attention to their readers; while it is often illusory attention in the form of public posts rather than direct responses and messages, the attention is nonetheless reflected and returned to them in the form of more followers and more sales. Followers and site hits are key indicators of audience size: the higher these numbers, the more agents, editors, and film producers will come calling.

By trading in not only texts but also in attention, these authors share their power with their readers. If a creator is seen as human, acquaintance, or friend, then they descend from their pedestal and walk among peers; they are no longer a divine genius, but "of the people" – a demotic figure. Readers find themselves thanked in acknowledgements, participating in collaborative writing projects, and influencing their favorite authors through discourse. The attention capital they exchange is no longer pedestrian, no longer "Oh, I recognize that author; I might buy their work in the airport"; now it is loyal, devoted, capable of conversion to pre-sales and special editions, to investment in new and riskier projects, and to purchases of remediations to film, comic, and game. These readers are fans, connecting more deeply in the original sense of the word: they identify themselves within the work and with the author, and so equate the author's success to their own sense of self. Such devotion results in highly devoted fan bases such as those of Neil Gaiman and Jasper Fforde, and Noelle Stevenson and Anna Todd, and their devotion converts attention to monetary capital for author, indie publisher, and royalty publisher alike.

The writerly practice that, as of yet, does not directly confer attention capital into financial capital is fanfic. While fanfic is a key indicator of a very deeply held fandom for a particular textual property, the attention is only one way: from that property's readers, to its text(s), to its publishers/producers, to its authors/creators. Few creators, particularly novelists, admit to reading fanfic of their work. Some cite concerns over intellectual property, fearing that if they were known to read their fanfic, they could be accused of stealing from it. Other authors, purporting an extreme level of ownership over their texts, express a desire to prohibit the practice entirely, as though it were a molestation of their characters. At best, some authors tolerate it, likely recognizing the levels of deep attention these very active readers offer to their texts, and the monetary gains that arise from such devoted audiences. Few, such as Hugh Howey, have ever actively encouraged fans not only to write fanfic but to sell it as well.

What these established authors, publishers, and many critics and researchers fail to recognize up to now is that fanfic is an emerging – or rather, re-emerging, since pre-copyright stories and texts could be considered fanfic – form of authorship. While twentieth-century media fan practices were largely those of a small and often derided subculture, twenty-first-century digital media has ushered in the era of the fan, from fan art to mash-ups to fanfics, which can dwarf their source texts in terms of both content and readership. In the hands of fanfic authors, the text becomes more than merely its source; it becomes a layered network of realized potentials, alternate universes, and fictocritical discourse. Unlike "original" texts (at least, those that aren't adaptations, sequels, prequels, re-imaginings, remediations, etc.), fanfics generally cannot stand on their own. Rather, they exist as intra- and intertextual nodes, textually expressing readers' desires, identities, interpretations, and explorations based on the actants and events of the source text. Often, they respond to what they see as lacking in the source: lack of representation, lack of creativity, lack of faithfulness to the characters, lack of *more*. In writing these texts, fanfic writers become authors whether or not they ever "file the serial numbers off" and choose to publish their writing. In writing, reading, sharing, and commenting on these texts, fanfic communities give voice to those who have historically been poorly represented in fiction, particularly women.[9]

These fanfic writers, however, continue to see their own work as illegitimate, and themselves as amateurs and hobbyists rather than authors. For some, this is preferred, as it gives them freedom to write what they want, rather than stress about professionalism, industry conventions, and audience responses. For others, however, this community-enforced perception of the hierarchy between author, publisher, and reader, and the ineffability of intellectual property rights, leads fanfic writers to unknowingly reinforce the patriarchal system that continues to ignore their voices. Other forms of fan art easily attain professional attention, respect, and monetary rewards without a whisper of unethical practice, including spec scripts and fan vids used as Hollywood calling cards, and art sold through Etsy and RedBubble. Fanfic, in contrast, persists in perpetuating the literary hierarchy established by twentieth-century publishers in order to protect their own income streams; nonetheless, its popularity and the numbers of readers and writers participating in its craft have grown substantially. As a form, it is already attracting corporate attention as a method of converting attention capital to financial capital, though no one method has yet proven successful. It is likely, however, that in the near future, fanfic will be monetized, and the fan writer will hopefully gain

---

[9] Also people of color, ethnic minorities, religious minorities, and LGBTQ+ communities, though these are less well represented and studied than women (Stanfill, 2018).

legitimacy as an author both from themselves and from the literary community at large. That these writers have not yet achieved that perceived legitimacy does not mean they are not yet authors; their creativity, craft, and ability to meet their readers' needs certainly define them as such, regardless of cultural or financial recognition thus far, as this Element has shown.

Authorship in Digital Environments

As noted in the Introduction, the preceding sections provide an opportunity to answer Marshall McLuhan's questions with regard to the evolving technology of the book, its production and distribution streams, and the environments in which author and reader connect over the foundation of common content:

> What does the new technology or practice *enhance*, *obsolesce*, *retrieve that had earlier become obsolete*, and *reverse into when pushed to extremes*? (McLuhan and McLuhan 1988; cf. Carolan and Evain 2013, p. 299).

In particular, what happens to the role of the author in digital environments with digital tools, including epublishing, ebooks, online publishing, and social media?

Digital media has *enhanced* the book, and the subsequent role of the author, in three key areas: the process of publishing, the variety in genre and form of the book, and connection to the reader. The path to publication has been streamlined significantly; rather than writing a novel, sending out queries, waiting for an agent to sell the text, negotiating through a series of editorial revisions, and then waiting again for a physical book to be set, printed, and shipped (all of which typically takes years), contemporary authors can publish their work online even as they write it (through blogs, social media, and online forums) or publish a completed text through ebook and POD. What's more, the text remains under authorial control, as digital files can easily be updated, upgraded, or withdrawn. With the costs of production (disregarding time and necessity of digital access) reduced to nothing, contemporary authors are no longer restricted to the narrow range of "marketable" books that royalty publishers can justify on a Profit and Loss Statement. Thus they may write the riskier texts, or simply those with a particularly niche audience, without concern that it will be shot down before ever having a chance to reach its target market. And as discussed throughout this Element, social media and online forums afford authors alternative means of connection with their readers, enabling the text to become a platform for a community of author and readers (who, as section 3 demonstrates, often become authors themselves) rather than merely a one-way method of artistic (and thus indirect) communication.

For books and authors, digital media *obsolesces* the traditional role of the royalty publisher, and thus the culturally embedded hierarchy of power between author, publisher, and reader, as well as twentieth-century notions of copyright and ownership. As the costs and processes of book production become digitized, crowdsourced, and democratized, new and established authors alike recognize the benefits to disintermediating the royalty publisher, at least in terms of epublishing: the author retains more control over the text and receives higher royalties on sales. As prominent authors such as Hugh Howey and Stephen King have pushed for hybrid royalty publication contracts – author-retained electronic rights, publisher-gained print rights – they have paved the way for other authors to do the same, effecting a paradigm shift in the distribution of power over the author-text-reader relationship. Authors now frequently bypass royalty publishers altogether, reaching their readers through Amazon, Lulu, Smashwords, and other e/ POD channels, or through new digitally shaped channels such as blogs, social media, crowdfunding projects, patronage platforms, and even fanfic sites. The growth of the last in terms of writers, readers, and mainstream visibility, in combination with the prosumer or read/write culture of the Internet, renders the rigid interpretation of copyright ownership obsolete to the point that forward-thinking Netizens devised a new system of rights management – Creative Commons – to accommodate the varied means by which contemporary artists and writers create and share art and literature online. While attitudes regarding copyright persist in their twentieth-century origins in fanfic, they have been interpreted much more loosely in other artistic realms such as fanart, sampling, and mash-ups; it is likely that the future of fiction writing will reveal similar shake-ups as well.

Digital practices of writing have *retrieved* a fluidity in terms of the definition of author, reader, text, and copyright. The democratizing nature of digital media and the Internet has created participatory spaces in which today's reader might be tomorrow's author, in which a text can be a playground. This is Ong's secondary orality at work: authors and readers are connected through the medium of written text, yet unlike print culture, this connection also enables interaction and textual permutations. It is no coincidence that one of the key methods of monetization for contemporary Internet writers and artists is patronage: primary oral culture models of remuneration for artistic practice are retrieved in secondary oral cultures. Likewise, the text gains a measure of flexibility, just as it once had in the oral storytelling ages of jongleurs and jesters: it can be reformed and added to, as Hugh Howey did when *Wool* took off, and it can be responded to and re-envisioned, as fanfic writers do. It can also take new shapes and forms, such as digital fiction, audio fiction, collaborative writing, locative performances, and more, as the cultural, technological, and monetary barriers-to-entry that were put in place by the few to "protect" and "elevate" art (according to a very narrow group's values) dissolve to afford the interests, talents, and voices of the many.

Pushed to extremes, the digital book and the demotic author currently *reverse into* the twentieth-century structures that still dominate the industry:

mimicry of the physical book, a hierarchical publishing tradition, and rigid protection of copyright. When fanfic writers such as Anna Todd and indie publishing successes like Andy Weir establish sufficient attention to monetize their success, they abandon their innovative practices in favor of established routes to traditional authorship: agents, royalty publishing contracts, print publishing, bookstores, and film rights sales. They pull to publish, and often nullify the platforms and texts from which they launched – sometimes to the dismay of the community that shepherded them to success in the first place. These reversions are evidence of a medium and an industry still undergoing transition. It is not quite clear what all the ramifications of digital technology will be on authors and their relationship to the publishing industry. At the very least, it seems the current trend toward disintermediation and fragmentation may hold, as evidenced by the growing number of indie publishers and writers embracing nontraditional platforms such as Wattpad and Patreon to practice their craft and interact with their readers. The demotic authors are often creating their own spaces outside of the royalty publishing chain, in which they can create, share, and commune. In particular, the rise of fanfic may have significant influences on cultural perceptions of authority, ownership, and creativity as future generations shift their attitudes based on exposure and participation in such. The future of the author could be as bound to repetition, mimicry, remediation, and re-interpretation as the past is, in the form of the oral storyteller's memorization, re-crafting, and re-telling.

For the publishing industry, the rise of the demotic author via mass authorship and a culture shifted to writing-based literacy represents a fundamental change in perception and practices with regard to authors, texts, and readers. The royalty publishing model dominated fiction in the twentieth century: publishers were arbiters of taste, presentation, edition, and price (Godine 2011, pp. 332–3). The book as an established form of technology cemented the role of the author as a romanticised genius, their words made permanent and unchanging; the need for capital and influence in the bookstore marketplace cemented the publisher's control of whose words could be distributed, and who could have access to them. In contrast, the digital book is "manipulable, dynamic and temporal" (Hillesund 2007, n.p.), making it a location of discourse and community, rather than permanence and authority. And if the book is not fixed, then the author is fallible, human – "of the people." The line between author and reader is imaginary and easily crossed. Money flows not toward the controller of the source text, but whomever generates the most attention related to it, whether the original text's author or a fanfic writer responding to it. In the digital age, the twentieth-century publishing model is obsolete, necessitating an evolved understanding of current cultural practices and the "constellations of authorship" afforded by digital media (Laquintano 2010, p. 487).

These constellations of authorship include not only the "professional" authors as defined by nineteenth- and twentieth-century systems (which devalued writing that was not legitimized by the royalty publishing process; Laquintano 2013), but also those who choose an indie, online, or fanfic publication path. Bourdieu's distinctions between "art" and "commercial/ bourgeois" works break down as the borders between author, publisher, and reader dissolve, with no gatekeeper or arbiter of taste save the author's own internal critic or their website of choice's content guidelines (Phillips 2014, p. 20). As long as an author can find and satisfy their audience, the legitimacy of their writing is irrelevant.

Further, coupled with digital media's multiplicity of capabilities, this dissolution of boundaries between legitimate and illegitimate writing (Dietz 2015) affords new grounds for creative exploration. The book is freed from both its generic and its physical constraints (Hillesund 2007; Phillips 2014): an electronic text can be shorter with no corresponding reversal in terms of cost-to-profit ratio, reifying the short story and novella; it can be much longer, as fanfics often are, reifying the serial and episodic novel; and it can be something more than the physical novel, such as hypertexts, interactive fictions, mixed media, collaborative novels, and more. The latter such efforts have primarily been conveyed outside the book or ebook altogether, in the form of online digital fiction, but some one-off experiments have appeared, including Iain Pears's iOS mobile app version of his novel *Arcadia*, and Caroline Smailes's eleven possible endings in *99 Reasons Why* (Thorpe 2013).[10] The future of the book, and by extension the author, is not grim, despite various publishers' laments; rather, it consists of a plethora of brightly lit pathways, all equally viable and legitimate, based on a culture that values writing, discussing, collaborating, sharing, and experimenting, in an environment that affords all of these elements to all participants.

The rapidity with which digital media evolves necessitates an almost continual call for more research in areas affected by it: translation, ebooks in different literary languages, publishing platform developments, cultural approaches to intellectual property laws, and author/publisher demographics with regard to whose voices are heard and amplified. This Element is by no means a comprehensive examination of the contemporary author. Rather, it has sought to examine the contemporary (and continually shifting) conception of authorship as affected by current technologies, while still straining against older perceptions of legitimacy. It has focused on the role of the author in the English-language publishing industry in the early twenty-first century, primarily examining fiction authors and novelists.

Storytellers have always been revered figures, from primary oral cultures, through our recent print culture, and continuing into our current secondary oral

---

[10] As a practitioner-researcher, I have also published interactive ebooks of my own: *The Futographer: A Hyperstory* (2016), and *The Pyxis Memo: On Resurrecting the Free Web* (2017).

culture. Yet all humans are storytellers, whether performing epic oral narratives, writing novels or television series, or simply communicating the events of our daily actions. We all have stories to tell, and we all have an audience. The peak of print culture saw the role of the author rigorously curated for purposes that benefited those in positions of power: where once the printing press had been used as a tool of revolution, by the late nineteenth and the twentieth century the print publishing industry had established itself as the arbiter of culture and cultural values, controlling whose ideas and works had merit, and whose weren't worth the paper they wouldn't be printed on. Of course, as with all endeavors, these values were highly influenced by the small cultural group in power: white, Christian men. Authors whose identities and/or works did not fit these narrow definitions of quality were discounted, devalued, and devoiced.

Digital media has the power to upend these relationships, and it is currently doing so by affording authors the ability to bypass the gatekeepers of culture, as it were. Voices that could only be heard when collected in large enough numbers are now amplified through indie publishing, reader communities, and fan writing. The role of the author is undergoing a process of democratization; while not all authors achieve an external success as defined by placement on bestseller lists or lucrative film rights sales, nonetheless all authors have greater opportunity to communicate directly with a willing readership via their texts. The demotic author emerges, using their digitally enabled power and their rich imagination to fill the infinite number of gaps left between rigidly and arbitrarily legitimized "professional" texts.

References

Aarseth, E. 1997. *Cybertext: Reflections on Ergodic Literature*. Baltimore: Johns Hopkins University Press.

Alter, A. 2017. Fantasizing on the Famous. *The New York Times*, December 21. Available at: www.nytimes.com/2014/10/22/business/media/harry-styles-of-one-direction-stars-in-anna-todds-novel.html [Accessed: September 29, 2018].

Alverson, B. 2016. Comics A.M. | "Roller Girl," "Nimona" Win Cybils Awards. *CBR.com*. [online] 15 Feb. Available at: www.cbr.com/comics-a-m-roller-girl-nimona-win-cybils-awards/ [Accessed: May 7, 2018].

Anon. 2000. Harry Potter: Meet J. K. Rowling. *Scholastic.com*. Available at: web.archive.org/web/20010413164034/www.scholastic.com/harrypotter/author/transcript2.htm [Accessed: September 29, 2018].

2008. Bestselling Books of the Year, 1996–2007. *Publishers Weekly*. [online] March 24. Available at: www.publishersweekly.com/pw/by-topic/industry-news/publishing-and-marketing/article/2110-bestselling-books-of-the-year-1996–2007.html

2011. Fan Fiction Demographics in 2010: Age, Sex, Country. *Fan Fiction Statistics – FFN Research*. [online] March 18. Available at: ffnresearch.blogspot.co.uk/2011/03/fan-fiction-demographics-in-2010-age.html [Accessed: May 7, 2018].

2013. I am Andy Weir, and I wrote "The Egg." AMA. *Reddit (AMA)*

2015. The Martian (2015) – Financial Information. *The Numbers*. [online] Available at: www.the-numbers.com/movie/Martian-The [Accessed: September 29, 2018].

2016. Young Adult E-Book Books – Best Sellers – July 24, 2016 – The New York Times. [online] *The New York Times* Available at:

www.nytimes.com/books/best-sellers/2016/07/24/young-adult-e-book/ [Accessed: May 7, 2018].

2018. Archive of Our Own. [online] *Archive of Our Own* Available at: archiveofourown.org/?language_id=en [Accessed: May 7, 2018].

2018. BBC Podcasts. [online] *BBC* Available at: www.bbc.co.uk/podcasts [Accessed: January 13, 2018].

2018. Pottermore.com Traffic, Demographics and Competitors. [online] *Alexa* Available at: www.alexa.com/siteinfo/pottermore.com [Accessed: May 7, 2018].

Asselin, J. 2015. 2015 Eisner Award Nominations Announced. *Comics Alliance*. [online] April 22. Available at: comicsalliance.com/2015-eisner-award-nominations/ [Accessed: May 7, 2018].

Bacon-Smith, C. 1992. *Enterprising Women: Television Fandom and the Creation of Popular Myth*. Philadelphia: University of Pennsylvania Press.

Barbrook, R., and Cameron, A. 1995. The Californian Ideology. Mute, September 1. Available at: www.metamute.org/editorial/articles/californian-ideology [Accessed: September 29, 2018].

Baron, D. 2009. *A Better Pencil: Readers, Writers, and the Digital Revolution*. Oxford: Oxford University Press.

Barthes, R. 1967 (1977). The Death of the Author. In: *Image Music Text*. New York: Hill & Wang, pp. 142–148.

1975. *S/Z*. New York: Hill & Wang.

Baverstock, A., and Steinitz, J. 2013a. What Satisfactions Do Self-Publishing Authors Gain from the Process? *Learned Publishing*, [online] 26(4), pp. 272–282. Available at: doi.wiley.com/10.1087/20130408

2013b. Who Are the Self-Publishers? *Learned Publishing*, [online] 26(3), pp. 211–223. Available at: doi.wiley.com/10.1087/20130310 [Accessed: November 2, 2017].

Benjamin, W. 1968. The Work of Art in the Age of Mechanical Reproduction. Translated by H. Zohn. In: H. Arendt, ed., *Illuminations*. New York: Schocken Books, pp. 217–251.

Benovic, C. 2016. How Do I . . . my Kickstarter Project? *Kickstarter*. [online] September 29. Available at: www.kickstarter.com/blog/how-do-imy-kickstarter-project [Accessed: May 7, 2018].

Bhaskar, M. 2013. *The Content Machine: Towards a Theory of Publishing from the Printing Press to the Digital Network*. London: Anthem Press.

Black, R. W. 2009. Online Fan Fiction, Global Identities, and Imagination. *Research in the Teaching of English*, 43(4), pp. 397–425.

Booth III, M. 2017. Writers: Why You Should (and Shouldn't) Start a Patreon. [online] *LitReactor* Available at: litreactor.com/columns/writers-why-you-should-and-should-not-start-a-patreon [Accessed: January 12, 2018].

Bourdieu, P. 1983 (1993). The Field of Cultural Production, or: The Economic World Reversed. In: *The Field of Cultural Production*. New York: Columbia University Press, pp. 29–73.

Bowker, 2016. *Self-Publishing in the United States, 2010–2015: Print and Ebook*. [online] Available at: media.bowker.com/documents/bowker-selfpublishing-report2015.pdf [Accessed: May 7, 2018].

Bradley, J., et al. 2011. Non-Traditional Book Publishing. *First Monday*, [online] 16 (8). Available at: journals.uic.edu/ojs/index.php/fm/article/view/3353/3030 [Accessed: January 17, 2017].

Bradley, J., Fulton, B., and Helm, M. 2012. Self-Published Books: An Empirical "Snapshot." *The Library Quarterly*, [online] 82(2), pp. 107–140. Available at: www.journals.uchicago.edu/doi/10.1086/664576 [Accessed: November 7, 2017].

Brandt, D. 2015. *The Rise of Writing: Redefining Mass Literacy*. Cambridge: Cambridge University Press.

References

Brennan, J., and Large, D. 2014. "Let's Get a Bit of Context": Fifty Shades and the Phenomenon of "Pulling to Publish" in Twilight Fan Fiction. *Media International Australia*, 152(1), pp. 27–39.

Brosh, A. 2013. *Hyperbole and a Half: Unfortunate Situations, Flawed Coping Mechanisms, Mayhem, and Other Things That Happened*. New York: Simon & Schuster.

Camacho, J. D. 2013. Is the E-Reader Mightier?: Direct Publishing and Entry Barriers. *Journal of Scholarly Publishing*, 44(4), pp. 327–339.

Campbell, J., et al. 2016. Thousands of Positive Reviews: Distributed Mentoring in Online Fan Communities. In: *Proceedings of the 19th ACM Conference on Computer-Supported Cooperative Work & Social Computing – CSCW '16*. [online] New York, New York, USA: ACM Press, pp. 689–702. Available at: dl.acm.org/citation.cfm?doid=2818048.2819934 [Accessed: February 27, 2018].

Carolan, S., and Evain, C. 2013. Self-Publishing: Opportunities and Threats in a New Age of Mass Culture. *Publishing Research Quarterly*, [online] 29(4), pp. 285–300. Available at: link.springer.com/10.1007/s12109-013-9326-3 [Accessed: February 25, 2016].

Coker, C., and Benefiel, C. R. 2016. Authorizing Authorship: Fan Writers and Resistance to Public Reading. *TXT*, [online] (1), pp. 20–27. Available at: openaccess.leidenuniv.nl/handle/1887/42717 [Accessed: February 27, 2018].

Coppa, F. 2006. A Brief History of Media Fandom. In: K. Hellekson and K. Busse, eds., *Fan Fiction and Fan Communities in the Age of the Internet: New Essays*. Jefferson, NC: McFarland & Company, Inc., pp. 41–60.

Crisp, J. 2013. One Year Later, the Results of Tor Books UK Going DRM-Free. [online] *Tor.com*. Available at: www.tor.com/2013/04/29/tor-books-uk-drm-free-one-year-later/ [Accessed: September 29, 2018].

Currah, A. 2007. Managing Creativity: The Tensions Between Commodities and Gifts in a Digital Networked Environment. *Economy and Society*, [online] 36(3), pp. 467–494. Available at: www.tandfonline.com/doi/abs/10.1080/03085140701428415

Darnton, R. 1989. What Is the History of Books? In: C. N. Davidson, ed., *Reading in America: Literature and Social History*. Baltimore, MD: Johns Hopkins University Press, pp. 27–52.

Derecho, A. 2006. Archontic Literature: A Definition, a History, and Several Theories of Fan Fiction. In: K. Hellekson and K. Busse, eds., *Fan Fiction and Fan Communities in the Age of the Internet: New Essays*. Jefferson, NC: McFarland & Company, Inc., pp. 61–79.

Dietz, L. 2015. Who Are You Calling an Author? Changing Definitions of Career Legitimacy for Novelists in the Digital Era. In: D. Davidson and N. Evans, eds., *Literary Careers in the Modern Era*. London: Palgrave Macmillan, pp. 196–214.

Dilevko, J., and Dali, K. 2006. The Self-Publishing Phenomenon and Libraries. *Library & Information Science Research*, [online] 28(2), pp. 208–234. Available at: www.sciencedirect.com/science/article/pii/S0740818806000223 [Accessed: February 25, 2016].

Doctorow, C. 2006. Giving It Away. *Forbes*. [online] 1 Dec. Available at: www.forbes.com/2006/11/30/cory-doctorow-copyright-tech-media_cz_cd_books06_1201doctorow.html [Accessed: May 25, 2016].

    2007. In Praise of Fanfic. [online] *Locus Magazine*, 16 May. Available at: www.locusmag.com/Features/2007/05/cory-doctorow-in-praise-of-fanfic.html [Accessed: September 29, 2018].

Dwyer, C. 2015. Ta-Nehisi Coates, Sally Mann, Lauren Groff Lead Shortlists For 2015 National Book Award. *NPR*. [online] 14 Oct. Available at: www.npr.org/sections/thetwo-way/2015/10/14/448053224/finalists-unveiled-for-this-years-national-book-awards [Accessed: May 7, 2018].

Epstein, J. 2008. The End of the Gutenberg Era. *Library Trends*, 57(1), pp. 8–16.

Escape Artists, I. 2018. Escape Artists. [online] *Escape Artists, Inc.* Available at: http://escapeartists.net/ [Accessed: January 13, 2018].

Evans, S., et al. 2017. More Than Peer Production. In: *Proceedings of the 2017 ACM Conference on Computer Supported Cooperative Work and Social Computing – CSCW '17.* [online] New York, New York, USA: ACM Press, pp. 259–272. Available at: http://dl.acm.org/citation.cfm?doid=2998181.2998342 [Accessed: February 27, 2018].

Fathallah, J. M. 2017. *Fanfiction and the Author: How Fanfic Changes Popular Cultural Texts.* Amsterdam: Amsterdam University Press.

Fitzgerald, A. 2010. Andrew vs. The Collective. [online] *Kickstarter* Available at: www.kickstarter.com/projects/magicandrew/andrew-vs-the-collective [Accessed: June 17, 2013].

Flegel, M., and Roth, J. 2014. Legitimacy, Validity, and Writing for Free: Fan Fiction, Gender, and the Limits of (Unpaid) Creative Labor. *The Journal of Popular Culture*, 47(6), pp. 1092–1108.

2016. Writing a New Text: The Role of Cyberculture in Fanfiction Writers' Transition to "Legitimate" Publishing. *Contemporary Women's Writing*, 10(2), pp. 253–272.

Flood, A. 2016. Good Night Stories for Rebel Girls Is "Dream" Kickstarter Success. *The Guardian.* [online] 25 May. Available at: www.theguardian.com/books/2016/may/25/good-night-stories-for-rebel-girls-is-dream-kickstarter-success [Accessed: January 12, 2018].

Foucault, M. 1984. What Is an Author? In: P. Rabinow, ed., *The Foucault Reader.* New York: Pantheon Books, pp. 101–120.

Freedman, D. M., and Nutting, M. R. 2015. *A Brief History of Crowdfunding Including Rewards, Donation, Debt, and Equity Platforms in the USA.* [online] Available at: http://freedman-chicago.com/ec4i/History-of-Crowdfunding.pdf [Accessed: January 10, 2018].

Gaiman, N. 2004. How to Survive a Collaboration. [online] *Neil Gaiman's Journal* Available at: http://journal.neilgaiman.com/2004/06/how-to-survive-collaboration.asp [Accessed: September 29, 2018].

    2008. Chris Riddell. [online] *Neil Gaiman's Journal* Available at: http://journal.neilgaiman.com/2008/03/chris-riddell.html

Garcia, A. 2016. Making the Case for Youth and Practitioner Reading, Producing, and Teaching Fanfiction. *Journal of Adolescent & Adult Literacy*, 60(3), pp. 353–357.

Garratt, S. 2015. The Martian: How a Self-Published E-Book Became a Hollywood Blockbuster. *The Telegraph*. [online] Available at: www.telegraph.co.uk/film/the-martian/andy-weir-author-interview/ [Accessed: May 25, 2016].

Gaughran, D. 2014. *Let's Get Digital: How to Self-Publish, and Why You Should*. 2nd ed. David Gaughran.

Gearino, G. D. 2005. Podcasting Takes Off. *The News & Observer*. [online] 22 Mar. Available at: www.newsobserver.com/lifestyles/story/2241709p-8621847c.html

Gibson, J., Johnson, P., and Dimita, G. 2015. The Business of Being an Author – A Survey of Author's Earnings and Contracts. [online] London. Available at: www.qmipri.qmul.ac.uk/news/2015/items/152262.html [Accessed: November 7, 2017].

Godine, D. R. 2011. The Role and Future of the Traditional Book Publisher. *Publishing Research Quarterly*, [online] 27(4), pp. 332–337. Available at: http://link.springer.com/10.1007/s12109-011-9242-3 [Accessed: November 7, 2017].

Goldhaber, M. H., 1997. The Attention Economy and the Net. *First Monday*, [online] 2(4–7), n.p. Available at: http://firstmonday.org/article/view/519/440 [Accessed: December 29, 2017].

References

Goodman, L., 2015. Disappointing Fans: Fandom, Fictional Theory, and the Death of the Author. *The Journal of Popular Culture*, 48(4), pp. 662–676.

Grumpy Cat. 2013. *Grumpy Cat: A Grumpy Book*. San Francisco: Chronicle Books.

Halpern, J. 2010. *Sh*t My Dad Says*. New York: Dey Street Books.

Harron, M. 2017. *Alias Grace*. (TV mini-series) Netflix.

Hellekson, K. 2015. Making Use Of: The Gift, Commerce, and Fans. *Cinema Journal*, 54(3), pp. 125–131.

Hellekson, K. and Busse, K. eds. 2006. *Fan Fiction and Fan Communities in the Age of the Internet: New Essays*. Jefferson, NC: McFarland & Company, Inc.

Hillesund, T. 2007. Reading Books in the Digital Age Subsequent to Amazon, Google and the Long Tail. *First Monday*, [online] 12(9). Available at: http://firstmonday.org/ojs/index.php/fm/article/view/2012/1887 [Accessed: November 7, 2017].

Hudson, L. 2012. Record-Breaking Kickstarter Turns Hamlet Into a Choose-Your-Adventure Epic. [online] *Wired* Available at: www.wired.com/2012/12/hamlet-choose-adventure/ [Accessed: May 25, 2016].

2014. The Crowdfunding Upstart That's Turning Freelancers Into Superstars. *Wired*. [online] 14 May. Available at: www.wired.com/2014/05/patreon/ [Accessed: June 21, 2017].

Hutton, C. 2015. Hall of Famers: Meet the Men and Women Who Changed Podcasting. *Paste Magazine*. [online] 19 Jun. Available at: www.pastemagazine.com/articles/2015/06/hall-of-famers-meet-the-men-and-women-who-changed.html [Accessed: January 13, 2018].

James, E. L. 2011. *Fifty Shades of Grey*. London: Vintage.

Jenkins, H. 1992. (2013). Textual Poachers: Television Fans & Participatory Culture. 20th Anniversary ed. New York: Routledge.

2006a. *Convergence Culture: Where Old and New Media Collide*. New York: New York University Press.

2006b. *Fans, Bloggers, and Gamers: Exploring Participatory Culture*. New York: New York University Press.

Jenkins, H., Lashley, M. C., and Creech, B. 2017. Voices for a New Vernacular: A Forum on Digital Storytelling – Interview with Henry Jenkins. *International Journal of Communication Forum*, 11, pp. 1061–1068.

Jones, B. 2014. Fifty Shades of Exploitation: Fan Labor and Fifty Shades of Grey. *Transformative Works & Culture*, [online] 15. Available at: http://journal.transformativeworks.org/index.php/twc/article/view/501/422 [Accessed: February 27, 2018].

Kaplan, D. 2006. Construction of Fan Fiction Character Through Narrative. In: K. Hellekson and K. Busse, eds., *Fan Fiction and Fan Communities in the Age of the Internet: New Essays*. Jefferson, NC: McFarland & Company, Inc., pp. 134–152.

Karpovich, A. I. 2006. The Audience as Editor: The Role of Beta Readers in Online Fan Fiction Communities. In: K. Hellekson and K. Busse, eds., *Fan Fiction and Fan Communities in the Age of the Internet: New Essays*. Jefferson, NC: McFarland & Co, pp. 171–188.

Kerley, C. 2006. Access to Supply Powers Demand – and First Sci-Fi Podcast Novel. (Q&A with Scott Sigler). *CK's (Innovation!) Blog*. [online] 26 Aug. Available at: www.ck-blog.com/cks_blog/2006/08/access_to_suppl.html [Accessed: May 7, 2018].

Kimball, D. 2012. Case Study: Robin Sloan Writes a Book. *The Kickstarter Blog*. [online] 16 Aug. Available at: www.kickstarter.com/blog/case-study-robin-sloan-writes-a-book [Accessed: May 25, 2016].

King, S. 2018. About 80. So Many Books, so Little Time. *Twitter*. [online] 30 Apr. Available at: twitter.com/StephenKing/status/990733616333443072 [Accessed: May 7, 2018].

References

Klems, B. 2014. How Hugh Howey Turned His Self-Published Story "Wool" Into a Success (& a Book Deal). *Writer's Digest*. [online] 23 Jan. Available at: www.writersdigest.com/online-editor/how-hugh-howey-turned-his-self-published-story-wool-into-a-success-a-book-deal [Accessed: May 25, 2016].

Knepper, B. 2017. No One Makes a Living on Patreon. *The Outline*. [online] 7 Dec. Available at: https://theoutline.com/post/2571/no-one-makes-a-living-on-patreon?zd=1&zi=ahnkb2w7 [Accessed: May 7, 2018].

Knobel, M. 2017. Remix, Literacy and Creativity: An Analytic Review of the Research Literature. *Eesti Haridusteaduste Ajakiri. Estonian Journal of Education*, 5(2), pp. 31–53.

De Kosnik, A. 2009. Should Fan Fiction Be Free? *Cinema Journal*, 48(4), pp.118–124.

Lammers, J. C. 2016. Examining the Pedagogic Discourse of an Online Fan Space: A Focus on Flexible Roles. *Mid-Atlantic Education Review*, [online] 4(2), pp. 2–12. Available at: http://maereview.org/index.php/MAER/article/view/19 [Accessed: February 27, 2018].

Landow, G. P. 2006. *Hypertext 3.0: Critical Theory and New Media in an Era of Globalization*. Baltimore: Johns Hopkins University Press.

Laquintano, T. 2010. Sustained Authorship: Digital Writing, Self-Publishing, and the Ebook. *Written Communication*, [online] 27(4), pp. 469–493. Available at: http://0-wcx.sagepub.com.unicat.bangor.ac.uk/content/27/4/469.abstract [Accessed: February 25, 2016].

2013. The Legacy of the Vanity Press and Digital Transitions. *Journal of Electronic Publishing*, [online] 16(1). Available at: http://hdl.handle.net/2027/spo.3336451.0016.104 [Accessed: November 2, 2017].

2016. *Mass Authorship and the Rise of Self-Publishing*. Iowa City: University of Iowa Press.

Le Guin, U. K. n.d. Ursula K. Le Guin: Answers to a Questionnaire (FAQ: Frequently Asked Questions). [online] *ursulakleguin.com*. Available at: www.ursulakleguin.com/FAQ.html#FF [Accessed: September 29, 2018].

Lessig, L. 2008. *Remix: Making art and Commerce Thrive in the Hybrid Economy*. New York: The Penguin Press.

Marom, D., Robb, A., and Sade, O. 2013. Gender Dynamics in Crowdfunding: Evidence on Entrepreneurs, Investors, and Deals from Kickstarter. In: *Academic Symposium on Crowdfunding*, *UC Berkeley*. Berkeley, CA.

Martin, G. R. R. 2010. Someone Is Angry On the Internet. *Not A Blog*, 7 May. Available at: https://grrm.livejournal.com/151914.html?page=3 [Accessed: September 29, 2018].

Matharu, T. 2017. From Writing Online to a Publishing Deal: Six Wattpad Sensations. *BookTrust*. [online] 23 Oct. Available at: www.booktrust.org .uk/whats-happening/blogs/2017/october/from-writing-online-to-a-pub lishing-deal-six-wattpad-sensations/ [Accessed: January 13, 2018].

    2018. From Wattpad to Published Author – My Journey. [online] *Wattpad* Available at: www.wattpad.com/story/30770504-from-wattpad-to-pub lished-author-my-journey [Accessed: January 13, 2018].

McCrae, J. 2018. Wildbow is Creating Web Serials. [online] *Patreon* Available at: www.patreon.com/Wildbow [Accessed: January 12, 2018].

McLuhan, M., and McLuhan, E. 1988. *Laws of Media: The New Science*. Toronto: University of Toronto Press.

Mediakix Team. 2017. How Many Blogs Are There in the World? *Mediakix*. [online] Available at: http://mediakix.com/2017/09/how-many-blogs-are-there-in-the-world/#gs.WIxaQjc

Miller, B. 2017. *The Handmaid's Tale*. [TV series] Hulu.

References

Miller, C. C., and Bosman, J. 2011. Amazon's E-Book Sales Pass Print Books. *The New York Times*. [online] 19 May. Available at: www.nytimes.com/2011/05/20/technology/20amazon.html [Accessed: May 7, 2018].

Miller, L. J. 2000. The Best-Seller List as Marketing Tool and Historical Fiction. *Book History*, [online] 3, pp. 286–304. Available at: www.jstor.org.ezproxy.bangor.ac.uk/stable/30227320 [Accessed: December 29, 2017].

2006. *Reluctant Capitalists: Bookselling and the Culture of Consumption*. Chicago: University of Chicago Press.

Murdock, C. J. 2017. Making Fanfic: The (Academic) Tensions of Fan Fiction as Self-Publication. *Community Literacy Journal*, 12(1), pp. 48–61.

Murray, S. 2010. "Remix My Lit": Towards an Open Access Literary Culture. *Convergence: The International Journal of Research into New Media Technologies*, 16(1), pp. 23–38.

2018. *The Digital Literary Sphere*. Baltimore: Johns Hopkins University Press.

Newman, A. A. 2007. Authors Find Their Voice, and Audience, in Podcasts. *The New York Times*. [online] 1 Mar. Available at: www.nytimes.com/2007/03/01/books/01podb.html [Accessed: May 7, 2018].

North, R. 2003. Dinosaur Comics. [online] Available at: www.qwantz.com/ [Accessed: January 11, 2018].

2012. To Be or Not to Be: That Is the Adventure. [online] *Kickstarter* Available at: www.kickstarter.com/projects/breadpig/to-be-or-not-to-be-that-is-the-adventure [Accessed: May 25, 2016].

2015a. *Romeo and/or Juliet: A Chooseable Path Adventure*. New York: Riverhead Books.

2015b. *To Be or Not To Be: That Is the Adventure*. reprint ed. New York: Riverhead Books.

O'Connell, M., and Kurtz, D. 2012. How To Make an Awesome Video. *Kickstarter.* [online] 3 Apr. Available at: www.kickstarter.com/blog/how-to-make-an-awesome-video [Accessed: May 7, 2018].

O'Reilly, T. 2007. What Is Web 2.0: Design Patterns and Business Models for the Next Generation of Software. *International Journal of Digital Economics,* [online] (65), pp.17–37. Available at: https://mpra.ub.uni-muenchen.de/4580/ [Accessed: June 16, 2016].

Ong, W. 1982 (2005). *Orality and Literacy: The Technologizing of the Word.* New York: Routledge.

Parish, R. 2015. In the Author's Hands: Contesting Authorship and Ownership in Fan Fiction. In: A. E. Robillard and R. Fortune, eds., *Authorship Contested: Cultural Challenges to the Authentic, Autonomous Author.* London: Routledge, pp. 107–120.

Pecoskie, J., and Hill, H. 2015. Beyond Traditional Publishing Models: An Examination of the Relationships between Authors, Readers, and Publishers. *Journal of Documentation,* 71(3), pp. 609–626.

Phillips, A. 2014. *Turning the Page: The Evolution of the Book.* Abingdon, Oxon: Routledge.

Powell, J. 2005. *Julie and Julia: 365 Days, 524 Recipes, 1 Tiny Apartment Kitchen.* New York: Little, Brown and Company.

Price, L., and Robinson, L. 2017. "Being in a Knowledge Space": Information Behaviour of Cult Media Fan Communities. *Journal of Information Science,* 43(5), pp. 649–664.

Pugh, S. 2005. *The Democratic Genre: Fan Fiction in a Literary Context.* Bridgend: Seren.

Ramdarshan Bold, M. 2016. The Return of the Social Author: Negotiating Authority and Influence on Wattpad. *Convergence: The International Journal of Research into New Media Technologies,* [online] p.1354856516654459.

Available at: http://con.sagepub.com/cgi/doi/10.1177/1354856516654459 [Accessed: June 29, 2016].

Reed, T. D. 2003. Jasper Takes Washington DC by Storm. *JasperFfordeFanClub.com*

Reid, C. 2014. S&S Acquires Anna Todd's After Series from Wattpad. *Publishers Weekly*. [online] 27 May. Available at: www.publishersweekly.com/pw/by-topic/industry-news/book-deals/article/62475-s-s-acquires-anna-todd-s-after-series-from-wattpad.html [Accessed: May 7, 2018].

Rhue, L., and Clark, J. 2016. Who Gets Started on Kickstarter? Racial Disparities in Crowdfunding Success. *SSRN Electronic Journal*. [online] Available at: www.ssrn.com/abstract=2837042 [Accessed: January 12, 2018].

Rice, A. 2008. IMPORTANT MESSAGE FROM ANNE ON 'FAN FICTION'. *Anne's Messages to Fans*. [online] Available at: www.annerice.com/ReaderInteraction-MessagesToFans.html [Accessed: September 29, 2018].

Robinson, J. 2015. How Noelle Stevenson Broke All the Rules to Conquer the Comic Book World. *Vanity Fair*. [online] 15 Jul. Available at: www.vanityfair.com/culture/2015/07/noelle-stevenson-nimona-lumberjanes-comic-con-eisner-awards [Accessed: May 25, 2016].

Rochester, S. 2012. Wattpad: Building the World's Biggest Reader and Writer Community. *The Literary Platform*. [online] 18 Oct. Available at: http://theliteraryplatform.com/magazine/2012/10/wattpad-building-the-worlds-biggest-reader-and-writer-community/ [Accessed: January 12, 2018].

Sandvoss, C. 2007 (2014). The Death of the Reader? Literary Theory and the Study of Texts in Popular Culture. In: K. Hellekson and K. Busse, eds., *The Fan Fiction Studies Reader*. Iowa City: University of Iowa Press, pp. 61–74.

Scribl. 2018. Welcome Podiobooks.com Authors! [online] *Scribl* Available at: https://scribl.com/info/podiobooks [Accessed: January 13, 2018].

Sigler, S. 2014. New Print Deal: Three Books with Del Rey. *scottsigler.com.* [online] 19 Mar. Available at: https://scottsigler.com/2014/03/19/new-print-deal-three-books-del-rey/ [Accessed: May 7, 2018].

2018. About Scott. [online] *scottsigler.com* Available at: https://scottsigler.com/about/ [Accessed: May 7, 2018].

Skains, L. 2010. The Shifting Author-Reader Dynamic: Online Novel Communities as a Bridge from Print to Digital Literature. *Convergence,* [online] 16(1), pp. 95–111. Available at: http://con.sagepub.com/content/16/1/95.abstract?rss=1

Skains, L., and Bell, D. (eds). 2018. *Normal Deviation: A Weird Fiction Anthology* Wonderbox.

Sloan, R. 2009a. Mr. Penumbra's 24-Hour Bookstore, the story. *robinsloan.com*

2009b. Robin writes a book (and you get a copy). [online] *Kickstarter* Available at: www.kickstarter.com/projects/robinsloan/robin-writes-a-book-and-you-get-a-copy [Accessed: June 17, 2013].

2009c. The Writing Life. [online] *Snarkmarket* Available at: http://snarkmarket.com/2009/2983 [Accessed: January 11, 2018].

2012. *Mr. Penumbra's 24-Hour Bookstore.* New York: Farrar, Straus and Giroux.

2014. Mr. Penumbra's 24-Hour Bookstore. [online] *robinsloan.com* Available at: www.robinsloan.com/books/penumbra/ [Accessed: January 11, 2018].

Stanfill, M. 2018. The Unbearable Whiteness of Fandom and Fan Studies. In: P. Booth, ed., *A Companion to Fandom and Fan Studies.* Hoboken, NJ: John Wiley & Sons, pp. 305–318.

Stapilus, R. 2015. Why Stephen King, J. K. Rowling, Joe Konrath and Others Are Switching To Indie Publishing – At Least On Some of Their Books. *Bookworks.* [online] 26 Jun. Available at:

www.bookworks.com/2015/06/why-stephen-king-j-k-rowling-joe-konrath-and-others-are-switching-to-indie-publishing-at-least-on-some-of-their-books/ [Accessed: May 25, 2016].

Stasi, M. 2006. The Toy Soldiers from Leeds: The Slash Palimpsest. In: K. Hellekson and K. Busse, eds., *Fan Fiction and Fan Communities in the Age of the Internet: New Essays*. Jefferson, NC: McFarland & Company, Inc., pp. 115–133.

Stevenson, N. 2012. TIME OF DEATH: 8:32 PM 4/26/12. *How Are You I'm Fine Thanks*. [online] 26 Apr. Available at: http://gingerhaze.tumblr.com/post/21882430339/time-of-death-832-pm-42612 [Accessed: May 7, 2018].

Tefler, M. 2018. Tefler Is Creating Sci-fi Stories. [online] *Patreon* Available at: www.patreon.com/user?u=3814558 [Accessed: January 12, 2018].

Thomas, B. 2007. Canons and Fanons: Literary Fanfiction Online. *dichtung-digital*, [online] (37). Available at: www.dichtung-digital.org/2007/thomas.htm

　　2010. Gains and Losses? Writing It All Down: Fanfiction and Multimodality. In: R. Page, ed., *New Perspectives on Narrative and Multimodality*. New York: Routledge, pp. 142–254.

Thompson, J. B. 2005. *Books in the Digital Age*. Cambridge: Polity Press.

　　2012. *Merchants of Culture: The Publishing Business in the Twenty-First Century*. 2nd ed. Cambridge: Polity Press.

Thorpe, V. 2013. Top Novelists Look to Ebooks to Challenge the Rules of Fiction. *The Guardian*. [online] 10 Mar. Available at: www.theguardian.com/books/2013/mar/10/novelists-ebooks-challenge-fiction-rules [Accessed: February 25, 2016].

Tian, X., and Martin, B. 2011. Impacting Forces on eBook Business Models Development. *Publishing Research Quarterly*, [online] 27(3), pp. 230–246. Available at: http://link.springer.com/10.1007/s12109-011–9229-0 [Accessed: February 25, 2016].

Timbuktu Labs. 2016. Good Night Stories for Rebel Girls – 100 Tales to Dream BIG. [online] *Kickstarter* Available at: www.kickstarter.com/projects/timbuktu/good-night-stories-for-rebel-girls-100-tales-to-dr/description [Accessed: January 12, 2018].

Tolkien, J. R. R. 1954. *The Lord of the Rings*. Allen & Unwin.

Tosenberger, C. 2014. Mature Poets Steal: Children's Literature and the Unpublishability of Fanfiction. *Children's Literature Association Quarterly*, 39(1), pp. 4–27.

Tushnet, R. 2017. Copyright Law, Fan Practices, and the Rights of the Author. In: J. Gray, C. Sandvoss and C.L. Harrington, eds., *Fandom: Identities and Communities in a Mediated World*, 2nd ed. New York: New York University Press, pp. 77–90.

Vadde, A. 2017. Amateur Creativity: Contemporary Literature and the Digital Publishing Scene. *New Literary History*, 48(1), pp. 27–51.

Wattpad. 2016. Wattpad. [online] Available at: www.wattpad.com/ [Accessed: May 25, 2016].

2018. Press – Wattpad. [online] *Wattpad.com* Available at: www.wattpad.com/press/ [Accessed: January 12, 2018].

WBEZ and This American Life. 2014. Serial Podcast. [online] *Serial* Available at: https://serialpodcast.org/ [Accessed: January 13, 2018].

Wecks, E. 2012a. Hugh Howey Interview Part 1: Science Fiction, Indie Writing, and Success. *Wired*. [online] 29 Mar. Available at: www.wired.com/2012/03/hugh-howey-interview-part-one-science-fiction-indie-writing-and-success/

2012b. Nathan Lowell's Solar Clipper Series. *Wired*. [online] 20 Jun. Available at: www.wired.com/2012/06/space-opera-without-explosions-nathan-lowells-solar-clipper-series/ [Accessed: January 13, 2018].

Weir, A. 2009. Creative Writings of Andy Weir. [online] Available at: www.galactanet.com/writing.html [Accessed: January 10, 2018].

2011. *The Martian*. Andy Weir.

Whedon, J. 2012. *The Avengers*. Buena Vista.

Wood, Z. 2017. Paperback Fighter: Sales of Physical Books Now Outperform Digital Titles. *The Guardian*. [online] 17 Mar. Available at: www .theguardian.com/books/2017/mar/17/paperback-books-sales-outper form-digital-titles-amazon-ebooks [Accessed: May 7, 2018].

Yates, J. 2011. *Cake Wrecks: When Professional Cakes Go Hilariously Wrong*. Kansas City: Andrews McNeel Publishing.

YouGov. 2015. *Bookish Britain: literary jobs are the most desirable*. [online] Available at: https://yougov.co.uk/news/2015/02/15/bookish-brit ain-academic-jobs-are-most-desired/ [Accessed: November 7, 2017].

Zheng, H. et al. 2017. An Empirical Study of Sponsor Satisfaction in Reward-Based Crowdfunding. *Journal of Electronic Commerce Research*, 18(3), pp. 269–285.

Acknowledgments

I would like to thank Eben Muse as a most kind and generous editor, and for his mentorship from the very beginning of my research career. I would also like to thank Samantha Rayner for her innovation and support of this series. For their contributions to various sections of this Element, I'd like to thank Astrid Ensslin and Kate Taylor-Jones for their feedback and guidance. For offering keen insights into the world of fanfiction, I'd like to acknowledge Murphy Parys, Charlie Wilson, and Meagan Lewis.

Cambridge Elements

Publishing and Book Culture

Series Editor
Samantha Rayner
University College London

Samantha Rayner is a Reader in UCL's Department of Information Studies. She is also Director of UCL's Centre for Publishing, co-Director of the Bloomsbury CHAPTER (Communication History, Authorship, Publishing, Textual Editing and Reading), and co-editor of the Academic Book of the Future BOOC (Book as Open Online Content) with UCL Press.

Associate Editor
Rebecca Lyons
University of Bristol

Rebecca Lyons is a Teaching Fellow at the University of Bristol. She is also co-editor of the experimental BOOC (Book as Open Online Content) at UCL Press. She teaches and researches book and reading history, particularly female owners and readers of Arthurian literature in fifteenth- and sixteenth-century England, and also has research interests in digital academic publishing.

About the Series

This series aims to fill the demand for easily accessible, quality texts available for teaching and research in the diverse and dynamic fields of Publishing and Book Culture. Rigorously researched and peer-reviewed Elements will be published under themes, or 'Gatherings'. These Elements should be the first check point for researchers or students working on that area of publishing and book trade history and practice: we hope that, situated so logically at Cambridge University Press, where academic publishing in the UK began, it will develop to create an unrivalled space where these histories and practices can be investigated and preserved.

Cambridge Elements

Publishing and Book Culture
Bookshops and Bookselling

Gathering Editor: Eben Muse

Eben Muse is Senior Lecturer in Digital Media at Bangor University
and co-Director of the Stephen Colclough Centre for the History and
Culture of the Book. He studies the impact of digital technologies
on the cultural and commercial space of bookselling, and he is
part-owner of a used bookstore in the United States.

ELEMENTS IN THE GATHERING

Printed in the United States
By Bookmasters